Journey According to .Re.

SNC

authorHOUSE®

AuthorHouse™
1663 Liberty Drive
Bloomington, IN 47403
www.authorhouse.com
Phone: 1 (800) 839-8640

Published by AuthorHouse 08/25/2018

ISBN: 978-1-5462-5683-0 (sc)
ISBN: 978-1-5462-5681-6 (hc)
ISBN: 978-1-5462-5682-3 (e)

Library of Congress Control Number: 2018909996

Print information available on the last page.

CONTENTS

——— 2015 ———

——— 2016 ———

2017

2018

PROLOGUE

To whom it may concern,

In this book I pray you get to experience me. Not the me you've heard about or who I present myself to be… but a true encounter with me and my life as I've experienced it thus far. If my story must be told, I prefer it be told in my own light according to me. It's not that my light may cast shadows on others around me, but that my light may provide a glimpse of the end of the tunnel for those of you who can't see. If I'm going to tell my truth, I have to tell it all.

For those of you who are reading this and feeling no hope inside, allow my testimony to remind you: God is LOVE, love is peaceful and everyday is just that, a day, and you can overcome it.

With love,

Serena Nicole Chapman

ACKNOWLEDGMENTS

From the bottom of my heart I thank every person that I've encountered who pushed me to follow my dreams. I thank every person who reminded me of my purpose when I struggled to see it. I thank my former Pastor, Joseph Wright, who saw a gift in me and gave me a platform to perform, inspire and write for our church. I thank the late Ahman Fralin for being the true definition of hope and faith, his life still teaches me lessons. I want to thank Ann Bodnar and Alexis Lanza who coached me through some of the toughest times in my life. Mrs. Lanza you actually kept my secret and made sure I felt safe after revealing it; Thank you. I thank Nikki Acevedo for awarding me the best story teller in 9th grade! Because of you I believed my stories could be told! I want to thank my grandmother Beulah Allen Cofield who loved me unconditionally and her love never changed. I want to thank my dad, Greg Chapman, for not only being a good father, but a best friend who cheered me on and stayed in my corner. I want to thank my mom, Jackie, for being one of my biggest inspirations and for never giving up.

Psalms 56:8

INTRODUCTION

The hardest and freeing thing I could possibly do in my life is tell you this:

I was abused from the age of probably 3, until about 14 years old. I share this with you only to tell my truth, but it's still painful for me. I came out about my abuse at 14. The sudden and drastic rejection taught me that opening my mouth had more consequences than keeping quiet. Opening my mouth showed me the value I had, and it wasn't much. I wasn't the only one being abused but I was the only one who came forward; so the abandonment taught me that no matter how much it seems like they love you, they'll leave you. I learned not to trust my own words. I believed that I would forever be a used napkin that people would crumble up and throw away. I disgusted myself to be honest. I felt like there was something wrong with me that I myself couldn't see but was obvious to everyone else. I learned how to transform into what I thought the people around me needed, it was exhausting. But, I couldn't stop. I was so desperate to know that someone could love me beyond whatever was "wrong" with me. I felt guilty all the time for not being perfect. I think I got into survival mode and stayed there. Days blurred, weeks, months, years all blurred together and I didn't remember parts of it. People would tell me stories about adventures we had together and I didn't know what they were talking about. I tried to get help through counseling, church and venting to whoever had an ear, but prayer and writing were the only escapes that slowed me down for a minute. Sometimes people really do want to be there for you, but if they can't even show up for themselves and be accountable, they can't show up for you. They could actually do more harm than good. My validation was based in others so I wasn't happy because it was impossible to be perfect all the time for every person I encountered. I grew up in the church but I struggled with God. I couldn't understand how a Being so powerful could love me without me earning it. I mean just in general, I didn't even want myself! I gave all my standards away....self-destruction was a true friend

Psalms 56:8

of mines. Please believe me when I tell you that I am not qualified to pass judgment on you. I'm only qualified to live in my truth…no matter how painful. I was screaming to be heard, but my sense of humor and bright smile caused my cries to fall on death ears. Sharing my poetry with you is sharing my diary. Sharing my poetry with you is sharing some of the darkest parts of me. But, I **Survived**. I'm still here. God carried me and I did not die. Although I am still imperfect and am still on my own journey, I know that God saves, He heals and He never leaves. I believe that my life is not about me, but about you reading this book… you are not alone, do you hear me? Don't give up on yourself, your goals, your healing, and don't give up on God! He hears you and He has a plan specifically designed only for you. If you don't know him, check him out for yourself, he loves me for real and he will love you for real too.

A Family of Six

A family of six
Who's love filled my heart
But because of one person
Has fell faintly a part
The family was tired
Of all of the games
Criticism and rudeness
Is just one person to blame?
A family of six
Which has now turned to one...
Because of impatience
And an old rusty gun
Poor evil soul
That now sits alone
Simply because their tortured heart
Has now turned to stone
The moral of this story?
Do I really have to say?
When your family is in need
Get on your knees and pray
Poor, poor family
A sad story indeed
They should of called on Jesus
Who can supply all their needs
This story is sad
But true,
Quick question,
In this position,
What would you do?

Psalms 56:8

Moment in Time

If I could go back
To a moment in time
I would definitely go
Back to when you were mine
The good times we had
Without a doubt outweighed the bad
But we let lies come between us
And that's pretty sad
Now that I think about it
It's ok with me
Why would we try to keep something,
That just wasn't meant to be?
I don't regret it happening
But I regret how it did
It's the problems that followed it
That I wish I could have forbade
Getting through life without you
It will be tough
It's always nice to have someone comfort you
When times get a little rough
And someone to stand up for you
When you've had enough

2007

Psalms 56:8

The Feeling of LOVE

In the twinkling of the moonlight
A glimpse of your beautiful face
Thousands of memories run through my mind
And my mind begins to race

Now you're looking in my eyes
A feeling my heart can't bare
It gently begins to rain
But we don't even care

And now we're drenched in water
But we still won't leave our scene
He says: I love you more than the stars and the planets
And everything in between

Now we're holding hands
As I whisper "I love you too"
With tears building in my eyes I say
"And I wanna spend my life with you"

And now the weather's cooling
And the warm air begins to chill
Not even the most exquisite word,
Can describe how he makes me feel

Now he's holding me tightly
As we lay where the butterflies fly
He kissed me and touched me so lovingly
As we watched the beautiful sun rise

Psalms 56:8

It STOPS with me

Lying in my bed
I'm just so confused
My mind is still racing…
What should I do?
It's hard to let people in
When you're constantly being hurt,
They build your trust up,
But it still doesn't work.
I mean why do they fake it?
And pretend like they care
Because when you need them the most,
They're not even there.
I'm so sick of crying
And falling apart
I am the innocent one
It was you from the start!
I just wanted to let you know
That it now stops with me
Whom the Son sets free,
Is free indeed.
I know you think you got me
And won this battle we had
You're probably laughing right now
Say "yea I got her bad"
Lord please forgive him
For he know not what he do,
He wasn't just hurting me
He was disappointing you too.

Psalms 56:8

Happy Birthday Mom

You may have thought I've forgotten
Or it just simply slipped my mind
You silly aging woman
I knew the entire time.
I knew this was your day
Special and so true
So now I take the time to say
Happy birthday to you
Happy birthday to you know
And so many times before
You're almost at the halfway point
So what are you waiting for?
Waiting for an opportunity
Or for that special chance
Get out there and live a little
Grab life by its hands
Grab it tight and swing it
As far as it can go
That life was full of the old you
And things you know longer know
You no longer know the past
It's gone but not forgotten
Just because you've changed
Doesn't mean your future's stopping
You may have though I've forgotten
Or it just simply slipped my mind
Happy birthday mommy,
Only until next time

Psalms 56:8

To Be Your Wife

You leave me speechless
My breath completely away
Every time I'm around you
I have no idea on what to say
You give me a sense of completion
Like together we are one
Never any dull moments
We're always having fun
And now you tell me,
You need me in your life
Out of all the women in the world
You want me as your wife?
I've never felt a love so real
I've never felt a love so true
Than the sweet, sweet loving
That I feel from you

To be totally honest
I think it's too good to be true
I had given up on love
and then I met you

Yes I'll be your wifey
Yes I'll be your friend
Yes I'll be with you baby
Until the very end
SNC

MONSTER

You terrible horrible Monster,
I'll never call you by name
Just, Monster, Monster, Monster,
For what you've done you should be ashamed
To me you're just a Monster
That's the only thing I see
You've broken ripped and torn,
All the innocence in me
I truly hope you're happy
Because you had the upper hand,
But oh, not anymore Monster,
I'm about to take a stand
You really used to scare me,
To where I couldn't move
That fear is changing to anger
And the determination to prove
To prove that you an animal
A Monster in every single way
Monster, Monster. Monster,
What else is there to say?!
I am a hero,
Because I did what was right to do
Now my daughters and their daughters
Won't have to face Monsters like you
You don't know how much I hate you
To the point I yell and cry
Because of you I'm confused and…
And can't understand why…
You probably think this is some fantasy,
Too sick and disturbed to be real
But what happens when it' time to step back into reality?

Psalms 56:8

Look at how you made me feel
You make me feel like nothing
Like my words have no effect on you
You Monster, even when I said no,
You always followed through
Ohhh how you how you make me angry,
Furious, burning hot mad
MONSTER
I hope you have it bad
Bad enough to hurt you
Just like you hurt me
Bad enough for you to see
What you really did to me
I was afraid to see you
You know, face to face,
I'm ready to look you in the eye now Monster,
And show you who's in what place
You took the best of me Monster,
Again and again
I didn't deserve what you did to me
But I refuse to let you win
One person can make a difference
All you have to do is stand
And if it's too big for you to handle,
Put it into God's hands
Yes I've been broken
And find it hard to live
But time after time
I always seem to forgive
I forgive you for hurting me
And for everything you've done
Yes I forgive you Monster
Because in the end I've really won

Psalms 56:8

You Don't Deserve Me

You don't deserve me baby,
I've been nothing but faithful to you
I find myself crying a lot more
And it's all because of you
You don't deserve me baby
I was too good for you
I did everything you ever asked me
And I did it all for you
I did everything you wanted
You didn't even have to ask
I would've done anything for you
Even the simplest task
Go ahead and leave me lonely
At least I won't die
I'd rather have you leave me
Than listen to you lie
Lie about your past
and everything you didn't do
Get out!
I do not need you
Even though you said you loved me
And without me there'd be no you
But that was just a selfish lie
And I believed it too

Psalms 56:8

I believed you cared
I thought you needed me
But now I realize
You don't deserve me
You don't deserve to be in my presence
And you definitely don't deserve my love
I thought I was your angel
Sent down from above
Through sickness and health
Til death do us part
Those words...
They came from my heart
But now that I think about it,
You've been bad for my health
I'm an independent woman
I can do bad all by myself.

These Words Unspoken

These words unspoken
But dwell so deep inside
These words that express my feelings
But I find ways to hide
Words that tell a story
Of an innocent teenage girl
Words that show her journey
And outlook on the world
Her mind is always racing
And beating to a different drum
She reaches her hand out for condolence
But no one has time to come
These words so deeply unspoken
That she's held in for a mighty long time
These words that hold true meaning
These words that acknowledge a crime
These words are like the wind
Felt but never seen
Dangerous, yet serene
These words are like a volcano
At any moment to explode
These words will leave an impression
Once they've finally been told
Forgiveness is a virtue?
Ways to forgive you must find?
With people stepping on my heart like a doormat
You want me to push that to the back of my mind?

Psalms 56:8

There's only your mind can hold
When you're constantly under attack
Your feelings and your emotions…
All at once begin to unwind
Unravel like a ball of yarn
That never seems to end
Every time you try to wire it up
It unravels again…

Even Though

Even though you promised
You'd grow old with me
I'll have to understand now
That it just wasn't meant to be
I know you're in a better place
So there's no reason for me to cry
But I just can't help myself
You didn't deserve to die.
If I could relive any moment
It would be our first kiss
That's the night you told me you loved me
But that's not all I'll miss
I'll miss that unexplainable feeling
I used to get when I look into your eyes
And the way you used to hold me, so close
Any time I cried
I'll miss your sinuating touches
The way your hands caressed my skin,
I'll miss your luscious lips becoming ones with mines
Ohh, why did it have to end?
You were my first and only love
My only love affair
I knew that if I needed you,
Without hesitation you'd be there
Our hearts, they were the same
Full and so complete

Psalms 56:8

Now without you in my life baby,
My heart, it skips a beat
Even though you promised
That you'd grow old with me
You're no longer here physically,
But your spirit lives in me

Forever Yours

Forever yours I'll be
Words cannot express what you mean to me
You walked into my life
And turned it all around
And ever since that moment
My feet haven't touched the ground
You keep me in the sky
Floating on cloud nine
I'd probably be able to handle you better
You weren't so damn fine
You are just so wonderful
Baby you set me free
I'm not worried about anyone else,
You're the only boy for me
You are my angel
Sent down from above
I thought all boys were the same
And then you showed me love.

If

If I told you that I needed you,
Would you stay by my side?
If I told you I was afraid,
Would you find a place for me to hide?
If I told you that I loved you,
What would you do?
Would your reply be thank you
Or I love you too?
Sometimes I think
That its too good to be true,
Nah, what am I saying,
I have trust in you.
Maybe it's me
Maybe it's not you
Sometimes it seems
Like we're two worlds apart
And the only thing keeping us together
Is our hearts
But what if one heart
Doesn't quite feel the way it used to?
Can that other heart take on the challenge
To complete something that clearly takes two?
What if I decide
That this is too much
Would you grab me by my had
And just tell me to hush?
Would you calmly take me on a stroll?
Right down memory lane
Would you show me the good times, the bad times and even some pain?

What if I said
I'm tired of this love game
In the end, one of us will be hurt
Then who will we blame?
Would you tell me that
Relationships go through ups and downs
And that it's your job to console me when I frown?
Would you tell me
That together we can make it through any trial?
Would you whisper "I'll always be here?"
And just hold me for a while?

I Think I Love You

Love is something special
Love is something true
I guess what I'm trying to say is…
I think I love you.
I know I really like you
I know I really care
I know that if you need me
I promise I'll be there
I hope that we will make it
I hope what we have will last
I hope that you stay strong by my side
Like you have in the past
Maybe we'll watch each other age
Maybe we'll watch each other grow
Maybe we'll watch each other change from teenagers to independent adults
Maybe you'll be the only love I know
I have faith in our future
I have faith in our dreams
I have faith in us staying together
By all means

I believe in you
I believe me
I believe in everything
That we think we could be
I think that you're special
I think that this is true
I understand what I'm saying now,
I'm saying I love you…

Psalms 56:8

Since I Met the Lord

Since I've met the Lord
My life has been changed
I've been broken, shaped, molded
And completely rearranged
All my pain and agony
I got on my knees and prayed
And with a little trust and patience
He took them all away
I can't keep your blessings a secret
I can't help but share it
I'm always quite excited
I hope the world can bare it
You've always been beside me
As far as I can see
And when I needed you the most
God, you carried me
You're incredible God
Who's name I'll forever exalt
You've fought all my battles
Even the ones that weren't my fault
So since I've met the Lord
I'll choose no other way
I'm finally here where I belong,
And I'll have it no other way

Psalms 56:8

Remorseful

I'm remorseful for what happened
And I wish it weren't true
But I know the pain your feeling
I've felt what you're going through
Everything happens for a reason
Everything has a cause
You have to understand that in war
Soldiers sometimes fall
This isn't an easy thing to conquer
You have to take it day by day
And gradually in time I promise,
God will ease the pain away
Death is a serious thing
Hurtful but so real
I've buried three close family members
And I'm just beginning to heal
Cherish every moment
With the people you know and love
Because at any given moment
They could be looking down from above
I've lost two of my three cousins in the last years
To violence and one to an car accident
All three of them were young and innocent
But death is something they couldn't prevent
Don't take life for granted
Do something you never thought you'd do
Don't let a moment pass
I'm remorseful for what happened
And I wish it weren't true
But I know the pain you're feeling
And if you need me I'm here for you

Psalms 56:8

In The Words of a Broken Heart

In the words of a broken heart
In the words of the tears I've cried
In the words of the ones I've lost
In the words of the times I've tried
Tried to hide my feelings
Tried to show little pain
Tried to forget the memories
And just tried to maintain
Maintain my true emotions
Maintain it from the start
Maintain the times we shared
Maintain my broken heart
Broken hearted once
But never quite like this
I honestly can admit
You one I'll really miss
Miss your sense of humor
And the way you make me smile
And how we could sit and just talk about nothing
And just laugh for a
In the words of a broken heart
In the words of the tears I've cried
In the words of the ones I've lost
Who didn't deserve to die

Psalms 56:8

I Like Being Me

I'm me
Simply me
What exactly
Do you see
When you look at me?
Cause
I'm not him
I'm not her
I'm not y'all
And I ain't them.
I'm just me
And you know what?
I like being me
I kick butt
And I like being me
I do hugs
I like being me
Not drugs
And I like being me
I don't drink
I like being me
I do the things
I do
And I don't have to explain
Myself to you
Because I accept the bad
And gave up what I had
I'd rather cry when I'm sad
Than blow up when I'm mad

Psalms 56:8

I realize
That I don't have to compromise
In order to live my life
I know that I've changed
My life rearranged
Sometimes it can be strange
But I deal with all the pain
But more or less
I'm me
Just simply me
And I'm standing in the mirror
And I like what I see.

Storm

Sometimes
I cry
But have no idea
why
If my life has a reason
Why do I keep facing
All of these bad seasons
I know my life is real
But I can't cope
With all the emotions I feel
I try
To live day by day
Thinking to myself
Everything will be ok
When I look at other people's lives
And compare them to mines
All of a sudden I realize
My life is close to fine
Close to fine but not good
I don't know
I live in the suburbs
But it seems so hood
My life is now different
But it's not better
But now I seem to be able to whether
Even the worse weather
And I know what I'm going through
Won't last forever
When I'm done facing this hell
Best believe I'll have an admirable
Story to tell

Psalms 56:8

Dare To Be Different

Stand up for what's right
Even if you're standing alone
Stand out; be different
Get out of your comfort zone
Why be like everyone else?
When you can just be you?
Stay above the influence
And do what best fits you
I hate it when people act out of character
Just tryna "fit in"
Hiding their true emotions
Because they wanna make a "friend"
March to the beat of your own drum
Don't stop; keep up the beat
The more you show your individuality
The more people will want to see
See what makes you different
See what draws them to you
See what makes you so unique,
She what makes you, you
Break the chains,
Stand apart
Ignore your mind
And follow your heart

Psalms 56:8

Ahman Fralin

Dear Ahman,
It's been almost a year
But still every time I think of you
I can't help but shed a tear

I HATED to see you go
God knows I wanted you to stay
But how selfish was I to want to keep you here to suffer
When with God I knew you'd be ok

I watched you in the hospital
And I never doubted that you'd make it through
But again, that was me thinking of myself
And not what was best for you

I've never been so close to you
That's why I wasn't ready for you to depart
Even though you're not here physically
You'll always have a place in my heart

I know your twins' heart's been torn
But like a rock he stands
He keeps CBC together
Because he knows you're in God's hands

Psalms 56:8

What stood out to most to me about you was your smile
Now I see that same smile in Amir
That smile represents
Freedom, strength, deliverance and very little fear

I love you, you were my cousin
I love you, you were my friend
I love you, you are my hero
I'll see you in the end

On Saint's Day

On the first you left me
But in a way I'm glad you're gone
Because now I know you're safe
In God's loving arms

Peacefully you came here
And so peacefully you'll leave
You had to spread a message
We all had to receive

Retrieve your testimony
Receive what you had to show
To show us that Jesus
Is the only way to go

You were a marvelous person
Perfectly created by God's mercy and grace
People were automatically drawn to you,
Because they could see the God in your face

I believe in you whole heartedly
I believe the words I see
Thanks for sharing your life
1-shot + 1 message = me

Psalms 56:8

Butterflies

Butterflies in my stomach
Chills run through my spine
Not just on occasion
I mean like all the time

Every time I see you
And I know that you'll be there
Every time I think of your fingertips
Caressing my short brown hair

I never believed in love
At least not at first sight
But my whole outlook on life changed
When I saw you on that night

Every time you kiss my lips
Butterflies
An instant image of your beauty
When I close my eyes

Butterflies in my stomach
I can't keep you out of my mind
I'll love you baby, forever
Even past the end of time

Psalms 56:8

Image

In the image of my beauty
In the image of my mind
In the image of my personality
That shows I'm one of a kind
In the image of my body
In the image of my shape
In the image of me walking by
You can't even concentrate
In the image if my soft brown skin
In the image of my luscious lips
The image of me taking your breath
Every time I swing my hips
In the image of my walk
In the image of my stride
The image of me holding myself with confidence
Carrying myself with pride
In the image of my fingertips
Pleasing your sweet caramel skin
Imagine your hard body caressing the softness of mines
Let the lusting begin
In the image of us wrapped in the bed sheets
Imagine me clenching your back so tightly
Because you're stroking in me so gently
Yet using all of your might
In the image of our pleasure
The image of our sweat
From all the lust building up
Since the day that we first met

My Place

Mama always told me
About God's great sacrifice
How he gave up his only begotten son
Whom we call Jesus Christ
Testimonies are often given
About how they found Christ in their lives
But that's just it,
Where's my place in Jesus Christ?
I finally have discovered
Who I am in HIM
I am his daughter!
His beloved!
I am! I am! I am!
I always thought of myself as a normal child
With a normal home
Well, have I got news for you
I'm an heir to God's throne
Through his strength and almighty power
I have the freedom to live
Every single hour
By his strips I am healed
Every sickness and disease and evil must kneel
Ask me once
I'll tell you twice
I'm his child
Who he loves so dear

Psalms 56:8

With him as my father,
I have nothing to fear
So devil if you're listening
My trials are already done
With Jesus as my attorney
The victory I've already won.

Nobody But God

It was nobody but God
That brought me to the light
It was only JESUS
Who held me late at night,

It was nothing but the Lord
Who planted the seed in my heart,
Which was his field
And watered it from the start

Thank you Jesus for your mercy
Thank you father for your grace
Thank you Lord for your kindness
Day after day after day

Nobody but my savior
That took my hand and guided in the right direction
It was only him that showed me…me
And not just my reflection

I love you Lord
No one else could have saved me
I love you Lord
I wanna be just like you

I love you Lord
You are almighty
I love you Lord
You're a dream come true

Psalms 56:8

For My Valentine

Roses are red
Violets are blue
I'd give anything
To spend my life with you

All my nights
And all my days
I pray that our love
Will last always
I loved you yesterday
I love you still
I love you valentine
And I always will

Being One

To think of us being one
In and out of time
The rush I get just remembering
Your hand holding mines

To think of us in the future,
Reminiscing about the old days
My love for you overflows
In oh, so many ways

To think of me being your wife
Raising our own family
I'll never know the feeling of being alone
Because you'll always be here with me

I love the way you hold me
So sweet and tenderly
I love the way you make me feel
Boy, you set me free

To think of us through the years
Fighting and acting out
But by the end of the day you'll be holding me
And we'll be loving again no doubt.

Psalms 56:8

2008

Psalms 56:8

Time

Time is moving quickly
But just not fast enough
I cannot wait to get out of here
Cause living like this is too tough

I wish I were a bird
So I could fly, fly free
High above the clouds,
Which is exactly where I wanna be

I wish I could believe
That trouble don't last always
I'm putting my trust in you lord
To get me through this phase

Mighty, mighty God
Awesome in every way
I'm sure things will work out for the best
If I just continue to pray

Psalms 56:8

Volcano

Like an angry volcano
I'm ready to erupt
All these years of lying and deceiving
Is really building up,
I thought you were my family
My own flesh and blood
But when the rushing waters were rising
You pushed me in the flood
Man, I should've known better
To even trust in you
You're just as much of a monster as he is
And you know what?
I hate you too
Lie, lie hoodwink
Fake, front deceive
I don't even know what I was thinking
To even let you convince me to believe
I'm not addressing y'all all together,
Nope. I'm coming direct
Cause if I don't come at you on a personal level,
It won't have the same effect
You know this isn't over
And I'll pray for you wherever you go
Cause you know what my father says
You're gonna reap everything you sew
Even though in time I'll forgive you
You'll still have to deal with my dad
So you better get it right soon
Or you'll have it pretty bad

Psalms 56:8

But I Decided Not To Cry

I decided not cry
When you said those things you said
I just stood there, in pure shock
With millions of thoughts running through my head
You told me I wasn't beautiful
And that I had a horrible smile
When you said those words with such sincerity,
My heart wouldn't beat for a while
No tears ran down my cheeks
When you betrayed me; your own flesh and blood
But man was my stomach turning,
I felt more worthless than I puddle of mud
But I decided not to cry
Not to even shed one tear
I wasn't even surprised when you said you were leaving
I knew you'd never be here
But oh my god did I want to cry
But I couldn't lose my faith
I knew the giant hole you left
My God would soon replace
Drowning in a river
Of all the times I've cried
I understand why the tears won't come now
Because the wells of my eyes have dried
Dried and fading slowly
So soon to be withered away
Actually I'm not even sure

Psalms 56:8

If they could bare another day
Lord I stretch my hands to you
I've done all that I could do
I'll just have to stand on your word
And pray that it comes to.
Father if you hear me
Please take this pain away
Give me strength and
Let me see another day

Psalms 56:8

Fear

Just as the dark shadows
Cast upon the sea
In the same exact way
Fear lives among me
Just as the rough waves
Crash against the ocean's surface
Is the exact same way that fear
Eats at me for no reason….

Psalms 56:8

The Deepest Feeling Yet

Drowning in a river
Of all the tears i've cried
I understand why the tears won't come now
The wells of my eyes have dried
Burning in a fire
That seems to never end
The burning can't compare
To the scars on my soul that won't mend
Battling in war
Dying from so many shots
Not even a thousand bullets
Could fill this empty spot
Living in a world
Where no one can be trusted
Lies, pain deceit,
The reasons my heart is busted
And I knew that things weren't right
But still I played it cool
I should have realized that it would be me
That would end up playing the fool
And all I did was give you my everything
But you demolished the foundation we made
Because you wanted to have your cake and eat it too
With a tall glass of lemonade
Angry like a mother bear
Defending one of her cubs
It's insanely crazy how you can hate someone
But still be so deeply in love
Raging like a bull
Fighting for every cause
But still it always ends up

Psalms 56:8

As me being the one to fall
And I saw my whole world crashing
But I kept trying to cover it up
I just couldn't find it within myself
To say enough is enough
Now I see you standing here
And my emotions begin to shake
Everything inside me starts to go crazy
And causes an internal earthquake
I finally lost control
My heart isn't beating I bet
Of all the things I've been through
This is the deepest one yet

Letting Go

Why are you leaving?
you really don't have to go
I know you have to go out and get experience in this world
I know! I know! I know!
Why would you get so close to me,
If you're not going to stay?
Why would you hold me when I cry?
And wipe the tears away
Who will I turn to now?
Big brother, you don't understand
You helped me face my monster
And extended your help and hand
You were the one that gave me comfort
When no one else was there
You told me to look to God
And you promised you'd always be there
Now you say you're leaving
And it will be a while before you get back
You can't just leave me like this
And come back into my life like "that"
Now my heart is heavy
And my soul is feeling weak
I really wish I could talk to you,
But my mouth, it just won't speak
I know I'm being selfish
I'm sorry I know I am wrong
Just promise you'll be back
And don't stay away for too long

Psalms 56:8

They'll See

They hated me; betrayed me
And now I'm no longer there
They hurt me; backstabbed me
And they didn't even care
They finally got what they wanted,
I'll pack my things and go
They'll probably never admit it
But in their hearts they'll always know
They'll know they took advantage of me
& left me cold without a breath
They told me that I'd never be anything
Even after death
But let me tell you something
Listen to the words that I speak
It's not that I was dumb
I was just a little naïve
I wanna tell you something
You will not continue to tear me down
Because if I call on my father
Everything will turn around
I don't need a family,
God is all I need
With Jesus in my life,
How can I not succeed?
So I'll let them go ahead
And do what they want to me
Cause I'ma be me with or without them
And in the end they'll see

Psalms 56:8

Monster part 2

So now we meet again
And I'm trembling in my shoes
I really want to run,
But my feet, they just won't move
Why am I so nervous?
I have the upper hand
But oh my, how you've grown
From a Monster to a Monster-man
It's funny how things work out
How they carry along
Because you're the one who's done the damage
But their telling me that I'm wrong…
It's not so much of what you've done
It's just the aftermath
You never had to face your mistakes
Or feel the people's wrath
No. I will not be subject
To your evil demands
No. I will not surrender
If anything I'll stand
I'll stand with confidence
Stronger than you'll ever be
With Jesus I'm like a mountain
Try and move me
You are not my monster
I am not your slave
What kind of control do you want over me?
What kind of power do you crave?

Psalms 56:8

Love

Love,
Yes I wrote this for you
Time
Is speeding what should we do?

How do you know its love when
Love and lust are so easily confused?
How do you know if they love you back
If you're making all the moves?

And then you make mistakes,
And I question things I should have known
If you cared so deeply for me...
Love would have bought you home...

I'm Hurt

I'm hurt because I love you
And you don't feel the same
I'm hurt and I feel stupid
But there's only me to blame
My mind is full of memories
And the times we shared
But now that it's all over,
Why do I still care?
I care because I needed you
And I thought you were the one
But who was I kidding,
You just wanted to have some fun
But now that it's all over,
Why am I not done?
I'm not done because I forgive you,
Even though you made me cry
I'm not done because you don't get it
Without you I'll just die…
I thought I was your baby,
I thought I was your wife
But now all of a sudden
You want me out of your life?
Out of your life completely,
Out without a trace
I still can't believe you had the courage
To say this to my face
The courage to leave me hanging
Completely in the cold
Now I'm stuck sitting here
With no one left to hold

Psalms 56:8

When you love someone
You put aside their flaws
Baby, you still don't get it
I loved you through it all
I loved you through the pain
I loved you through the hype
I was the one up with you honey,
When you couldn't sleep at night
I've made up my mind,
I just won't let you go
And I don't care what you say!
You're the only love I know!
Please don't leave me baby
Please don't go like this
Isn't there anything,
About me that you'll miss?

Miracles

I believe in miracles
Just because I know they can come true
Jesus, you're my miracle
I believe in you
I was falling quickly
Too fast for me to even understand
And when I thought it was all over, I looked up
And saw your unchanging hand
Even when I ran from you
You never left me astray
Oh Lord, what was I thinking?
I almost threw my miracle away
Sometimes I sit back and wonder,
What could you want with a fool like me?

Alone At Last

In the sensation of the sun rays
Warming my sugar brown skin
Every worry and struggle in my life
All at once seem to come to an end
Standing in the clear ocean
Letting the waves carry the stress away
It's amazing how such an exquisite site
Could leave you speechless all day
Alone and lost in my thoughts
There's no place I'd rather be
The fish keep swimming close to my feet
And their fins are tickling me
Standing completely motionless
Watching the beautiful sun rise
Constantly, I've been arriving here at six
To the place where my heart and soul lies
An indescribable feeling
I feel when I'm standing here
I want to stay here forever
But my time to leave is growing near
Leaving is always my trouble
Everything screams "Don't go!"
But just the memories will bring me comfort
And this is something I truly know
Serenity

Psalms 56:8

Identity

Body, soul, and spirit
Are all a part of me
But what stands out most to God
Is my spiritual identity
Physically I am a woman
That works hard for days and days
Mentally I am a teenager,
Trying to part from my childish ways
Spiritually I am an ambassador
For my savior Jesus Christ
When the devil asks me once,
I make sure I tell him twice
I stand out because I'm different
I stand out because I'm blessed
Now answer me this one question,
What makes you different from the rest?

Deeper Than the Skin

If you only knew
That it's deeper than the skin
Then probably you wouldn't hurt me
And I wouldn't have to pretend
Pretend that I'm not tired
Of playing this horrible game
Pretend that my shoulders aren't heavy
From carrying all of the blame
Stop stepping on my heart
I have never stepped on yours
Stop turning your back on me
And leaving my spirit so sore!
Do you forgive someone…
Whose only caused you pain?
How do you forgive someone…
That drowned you in the rain?
What is it that you do
When they try to fake it like it wasn't so
Do you go ahead and keep pretending
Even though inside you know that you know?
Don't misunderstand me,
I'm not the same person you've always known
It's funny cause you grow up a lot
When you spend your time alone

Psalms 56:8

Tick, tick, tock
Life will still go on
Like a never ending beat
To a never ending song
If they only knew
That it's so, oh so much deeper than the skin
There's no way they would've hurt me,
And that's how the story ends

Stimulating Touches

Simulating touches
My secret true desire
Just your warm embrace
Sets my soul on fire
Something's not quite though,
I'm afraid to let him in,
I'm sorry I just can't trust him
My heart can't take being hurt again
But my heart knows that if he's the one I can feel it's true
But girl he's gotta straighten up
Or I don't know what I might do
Lost in confusing thoughts
Running crazily through my mind
Wishing that I could relive the old days
Even if only one more time
In the end I know we belong together
A feeling like this just has to be real
It's just a work in progress
And that's honestly how I feel

Caramel Skin

Caramel skin
Perfect in design
Everything you do
Stays on my mind
Your eyes are like a tunnel
That leads to a new world
I'm actually still in shock
I can't believe that I'm your girl
You know you drive me crazy
Especially that smile
When you smile and tell me you love me,
My emotions go wild
You walked into my life
And flipped it all around
And ever since that moment
My feet haven't touched the ground
You keep my head in the sky
Floating on cloud nine
I'd probably be able to handle you better
If you weren't so damn fine
You're just so wonderful
The only person I see
I'm not worried about no one else
You're the only boy for me
Baby you're my angel
Sent down from above
I thought all boys were the same
And then you showed me love
They say a boy worth your tears
Won't make you cry
But how will you know its love?

Psalms 56:8

If he hasn't wiped them from your eyes
Wiped your tears and held you
Ever so close to his heart
Rubbing his fingertips through your hair
And whispering "we'll never be apart"
I can always be myself around you
You accept me for me
I feel like when I'm with you
I can be who I want to be
I can do anything with you
I can just play around
I can do something completely crazy
And you'll catch me before I hit the ground
Caramel skin
So sweet and divine
My love for you will last
Even past the end of time

Dear Love

Dear Mr. Love,

I can't believe I'm still wasting my breath on you, but there's something I feel I need to get off my chest.

Dear Mr. Heartbreaker,

It's really strange that you would run to nothing…when you had the heart of the best

Dear hinderer,

You've had many chances to prove yourself; you just couldn't pass the test

Dear Mr. Special,

Maybe not today, tomorrow, or the next year, but you will realize what a ridiculous choice you chose.

Dear Mr. Incredible,

By the time you come running back to me; my love for you will be old.

Dear Mr. Confused,

When you have something good hold on to it, but I guess that's something you didn't know

Dear Mr. Unexpected,

In the many lonely, regretful nights you still have to come I wish you the best

Dear Love,

I'm glad to finally get that off my chest

Love always,

Freedom

Mothers

Mothers of the church are like
The star at the top of the Christmas tree
They're like the love that manifests in me
Because they came from slavery to poverty
To exceeding the highest limitations
They're one of the few women that stood against
The curse of generations
Because of their faith, trust and hope that they have in their savior,
I realize that I too could have God's great favor
Because of the way they made their unmovable stand
I finally understand those triumphed words of "Yes We Can"
Because these mothers are like a weeping willow tree
Steadfast, unmovable, breaking boundaries
When a mother prays for you, she's foreshadowing victory
Because of you, I know I can succeed,
I love you mothers, and that's not even half
Of the effect you have in me

Psalms 56:8

Dear Diary

I saw him again today. No I didn't speak. How could he do something like this to me? My God, I feel so weak. Yesterday on my way to class I saw him in the hall, my legs went numb I couldn't move, I just knew that I would fall. I understand completely that he's finished and doesn't care how I feel, he just mad cause he ain't get none, come on let's be real. I don't need him to tell me how beautiful I really am. I'm growing up, I can't babysit it's time for a young man. He wasn't benefiting me, so I had to cut all ties, I don't know about you diary, but I can't build a relationship off lies. He took my love for granted and now there's none left. Oh, well diary, I can do bad all by myself.

Pain

Does the pain ever stop?
Will it ever go away?
Or will my heart drip blood from this cut…
Each in everyday
The more and more I think back on it
The stupider and more hurt I feel
The drips from my cut fall quicker
Cause I realize you were never real
Time has been so mean to me
Especially when no one else is around
The hands move slower and slower
Until they no longer make a sound
Take back those knife cutting words
Come back let's have a fresh start
Please, please I'll give anything
To bandage this hole in my heart
All I do is sit around
Eyes puffy from the tears of reality
But I guess that's the price you pay
When you love someone unconditionally…

2009

Psalms 56:8

More than Conquerors

To conquer something is to overcome it by force.
It's not to give up, run away or quit the course
It means to stand strong, claim victory
And know that the Lord has got your back
It means to plant your feet firmly into the ground
Because the enemy is bound to attack
But the Lord's grace is sufficient
In other words, he's as much as we need
So stop trying to fight your own battles
Take the Lord's hand and let him lead
Know, in all things we are more than conquerors
Through him that loved us. Know that
There is nothing, absolutely nothing that can separate
Us from the love of Jesus
I'm grateful for the things you've done
Because of you the battle's won
You died for me with no regrets
Thank you Lord, I'll never forget my hero
Jesus Christ
My hero

Psalms 56:8

Race

Sticks and stones
May break my bones
But words are worse
They murder my soul
If we supposed to be "brothas"
And if we're one is a fact
Then why do you label me with harsh stereotypes
And expect me to be cool with that?
When you act the same way I do
And your race's criminal record fits mine to a "T"
But of course in a crooked, twisted world somebody has to be the weakest link
And you chose me
I refuse to let the pigment of my skin define my true identity
I promise myself to exceed, to go beyond
All the labels the world had pressed upon me
You say that it's the past
And that slavery days are mad old
Then why you still calling me a "nigga"?
Like you still gotta be in control
"oh relax" you say
"They just words they ain't even real"
Well what if I started calling you
Cracker, Spic or Chink, how would that make you feel?
"Chill out yo" Nigga is just an informal way
Of saying my brother what's good,
Yea, and when I say Cracker, I ain't being racist,
I'm just speaking of someone who ain't never been to the hood

Psalms 56:8

I refuse to be a part of the black stereotypes
I refuse to allow myself to get mixed up
In all the shooting, killings, drugs
And all the hype
The problem isn't that we're different
It's the similarities of our face
Well, that because we have one little thing in common,
We're one race; The human race.
Word

When I Die

When you bury me, bury me in an upright position
Cause laying me down would only show I've had enough
See me? I'm like the road runner
I can't stop; I never give up
What's wrong? You seem a little quiet
Did you think my death would slow me down?
Nah, cause now my words will haunt you
Submerging you deeper and deeper until you drown
The more you try to condense me
In the words of Maya Angelou "Like air I'll rise"
You seem a little restless now,
Is it because you know I won't compromise?
I guess you can say I'm in my bag,
Or my sock, or whatever you wanna call it
Cause I spit words like fire
That'll have you stumbling like an alcoholic
Don't misunderstand me
I ain't trying to boast or build myself up
It's just, I worked mad hard to get where I'm at
And homie I'm Tonka tough
It ain't even about the war
It's about the soldiers
And y'all out here shooting and killing each other all crazy
That's drawin', I ain't even gon' hold you
The only way we gon' make it
Is if we stand together and unite
YOUR BROTHER IS NOT YOUR ENEMY

So, stop believing all the hype
Yo, so when I die,
Bury me standing straight up
Cause Ima fight for ever,
I don't know about you, but I can't give up

Stroke

It's crazy cause it's like
You're trying to play psychological games on my mind
You caught up though, cause you wanna know what makes this one different
You wanna know why I'm not chasing you this time.

You wanna be cool so bad,
Ok, now I'm ready to be cool
But when I approach you, you can barely speak
You try to play me out like I'm a fool

Alright I understand
I'll take one for the team
I'm used to being the criminal even though
I clearly the victim in this scene

Why you working so hard to try and manipulate and
Seduce my mind into thinking that I'm the one who's at fault?
I'm not the one who used and took advantage of you,
Oh, my bad, it's only called using if you get caught

Now that it's over and done with
I'll right this down as another page in my notes
And I will forever remember
That you caused my first stroke
Heart Broken

Best Friend

LOOK AT ME
Can't you see I've had enough?
My body is broken, worn down,
And weak from all these cuts
Why you still tryna hurt me?
After all the things I've been through
Why are you still tryna cut me?
Can't you see there's no more room?
I'm tired of being cut
I'm tired of bleeding pain
I swear its wounds like this,
That could make a person insane
And you want me to bare the shame?
Um…is it cause you can't handle all the blame?
Or you just tryna not to tarnish your good name?
Ok, your name is already trash
Oops! That what you get for being fast!
So why you working so hard to keep your name clean,
When it's already broken like glass
Oh, yea, you sophisticated
And carry yourself with class…psych!
Now who's getting the last laugh?
All I got to say is,
Ha haha you funny
I'm acting childish?
You got it twisted honey.
How am I the one wrong
When you stabbed me in the back
And you feel as though you're the victim?

Psalms 56:8

Man, get out my face with that
We was supposed to be sisters best friends
Right hand chicks
But you left me by the waist side for an opportunity
To get some dick
After all the crap I did for you,
I held you down and even took your blame
And you played me out for a dirty lame nigga
And you ain't even know his last name.

Lucky

I learned something about myself today,
I'm more special than I thought I was…
Cause I met you on a cold day,
But you turned it into a spring day
You came around and made the snowflakes,
On my heart go away
You taught me that life is what I make it,
You told me that anything is possible through God
I wanted to make a quick left turn
But you said it would be better to make a right turn
But, I went left anyway, and that's how I got burned
You said, don't go back that that, that way only leads to heart ache,
But I stuck to my choice….which caused me to cry until I lost my voice..
You said love could be real if I let it…and that life could be amazing if I
wanted it to be.
You said that you would hold me…
But being held was something that was new to me…
But then you grabbed me a pulled me close, ugh,
You smelled so sweetly
Everything you promised you did and everything you said you showed
I love you like a fat kid loves cake
And I really, really love ice cream cake
But cake can't make my heart shake!
I learned something about myself today
I'm more special than I thought I was…
Cause I met you on a cold day,
But you made it a spring day,
You made your way into my heart
And that is where you'll stay

Psalms 56:8

Warning

I know what you're thinking,
Here she comes with her motivating words,
And her inspirational rhymes
Actually, no, not this time
I've come by with a warning
To warn the generation of how far we've gone astray
Listen to me, I'm telling you that Jesus said to just
STOP! Turn around! You're going the wrong way!
What? You think just because you think you're getting away with your
sins you're smart and wise?
How do I put this?
If you compromise, before you know it you'll be living lies.
& not lies to the world because after all there's no such thing as lies in a
place of lies.
Come on, seriously. Start looking through your spiritual eyes.
Because everything that seems right and looks right, isn't always true.
You've got to stop looking at the flesh and start looking through
Because the battle is not against flesh and blood,
It's against rulers and principalities, and powers
And spiritual wickedness in high places
I see y'all looking at me a little funny now,
Wipe the shocked look off your faces
Don't you know that we are living in a world full of sharks and snakes and
wolves in sheep's clothing?
I don't know about you but I've got my sword, what are you holding?

Psalms 56:8

If you know Jesus like you say you do, then you know
That he's the God of eternal life
Now's the time for healing and deliverance,
Come on! Choose life.
We are honestly living in the last days now y'all
Just read revelations, the prophecies are coming true….all I know is, I wanna be ready.
What's your choice? What are you gonna do?
When they say tomorrow ain't playing
There is no LOL at the end. So what's your choice going to be?
Live for God and Die to sin.

Love Is

I love you.
And I'm absolutely sure this time.
I know because I realize what love is.

Love is, a downpour of emotions. Some good, some bad, some overwhelming, all of which we don't understand but we can't let go.

I know you probably don't believe me, but I know that I love you because love is….is when you become one. What you feel I feel. When you cry I cry (which all of these things you do, do). When I smile you smile… even when you don't want to.

Love is something that flows deep within your veins and makes its' way to your heart…where it is then transferred and manifest throughout the rest of your body.

Love is when we've had a terrible fight and I hate you for it but we kiss…and when we kiss I forgotten everything that's happened. For that moment, for that little flicker in time, there was just me and there was you and everything was ok. For that very second, the world wasn't beating against…our love.

That's when it hit me, I mean that's when I noticed I loved you.

Omg, I love you with all my heart and soul, I do. Because even though we've had our bad memories and our difficult times, where I questioned my love for you and wondered what you were thinking to have even chosen me, we met, I mean our eyes and everything made sense, in some weird crazy way, it made sense.

Because I didn't choose you and you had no idea it would be me, but we're here together; one unit. Not collaboration but a collage of a bunch of different you's and me's making perfect harmony. But if one little piece goes missing…it would be nothing…we'd be nothing.

You see, I love you because even when I hate you, I mean when you really get on my nerves …I miss you. And when I want you to go you stay, because you know I don't really wanna be alone. I just love you.

Psalms 56:8

Psycho

It hurts cause I wonder what they really think of me…

And when I try to explain myself, why don't they believe me? I tried to tell them but instead of listening they told me that I needed to just fess up to my own mistakes…What? My own mistakes?

I take on the burdens of my own mistakes plus get crushed by the burdens that aren't even mines!!

I'm going to drive myself into a mental institute they tell me….me? Me! I'm the one making myself this way…Am I crazy or psycho to them? That's the way they make it seem.

I'm telling you the truth! Listen to me! I never lied before, trust me it's the least you can do…

He touched me…violated me, hurt me and you know he did. Why would I lie about that?

How can you not believe me or help me when I can't even sleep at night? How can you say you believe me when I'm around but when I'm gone put it out of sight?

I wish I never told you, or any of you, because of all the pain you put me through. How dare you call me a liar! You weren't there it wasn't you!

After all the things I've experienced from this test that God is putting me through is that, I know if something is not right, it's wrong. I also learned that if I don't like something there's a reason.

This girl's not who you think she is; she's not real. She's a fraud, false advertisement; she's going to hurt you! Hurt me, she's dangerous!

I know because I've seen with my own eyes. I've figured it out; I know it's true.

Oh yea, wait, you don't believe me. It's ok though, I'm not surprised it's nothing new.

But when all of this smacks them in their face what are they gonna do? Crowded around me and tell me they've always believed me but just doubted for a few?

And do you know what I'll have to say to that?

Psalms 56:8

Nothing to drastic, just a big SCREW YOU!

It hurts cause they think I'm not good enough to tell the truth….but they don't have a heaven or hell to put me in

As long as I know who I am and who I can be, I'll make out just fine in the end.

4+

And here I am, still tryna figure out this whole life game. Stuck on stupid because so many thing are going on that I can't...I don't understand..
What am I missing? Cause for real I have no clue.
How am I wrong? I'm always wrong. Why am I wrong? What did I do?
I'm trying to figure out my mind, I am
But I'm so confused.
I'm trying to sing to an upbeat tempo
But all that keeps coming out is the blues
I'm trying to get past my past,
But...my God I feel so used
I guess I lost my confidence because in everything I do, I fear I'll lose.

I'm tired of playing the blame game
The, you pick up the slack and take the shame game
The even though you're innocent let's throw you in the flame game
No! I'm done with those games

Now it seems to me, that I was put here to be alone.
My whole thing is, I've never taken loneness to fondly.
If I'm supposed to be standing out; leading the crowd in the right direction,
Why am I being pounded down by so much pain, disappointment, emptiness and fear?
Why are you accusing me and not asking me if you weren't even there?
It's funny because you said you loved me, but when I needed you most you were nowhere near....
I believed in you and that's partially the reason I'm still sitting here...

Psalms 56:8

I'm tired of going through this love circle
The, me getting played like Urkel circle
The no freedom no power, slavery, color purple circle.
The, you go first and I'm last murder circle
Nah, I'm done with those circles.

I don't know where I'm supposed to go from here
I wanna know my purpose.
My purpose for living this life….
But no one's leading me in the right direction
As a matter of fact, no one's leading me anywhere
If I'm a leader, what will I lead? My purpose? What is it?

Forget it.
Man cause I really don't get this, it's not that I'm impatient though,
It's my family and closure that I miss.
I wanna live for God but, I'm tired of being dissed.

Now, I know I shouldn't feel like this,
Confused and everything,
But life these days is like a chaotic fun house…
I can't see my reflection in any of the mirrors I'm looking in
For I desperately don't want to be this way
I'm begging for someone to fight my case!

Jesus, I'm sorry I don't mean it…
But my heart has been erased…
Have I traveled so far from you that I can no longer see your face?

What have I done? I've stepped of track and lost my place

Psalms 56:8

I remember God saying: For you a chosen generation, a royal priesthood....
just cause I grew up here..doesn't mean I'm a product of the hood
I'm from the God comes first like Tye Tribbet said "The good in the hood,
hood.

Jesus I'm sorry for disrespecting you...
I'm pulling down my hood...

Listen, in my young life I've realized that there's nothing more important
than a relationship with God.
Because for real, he never gave up on me...he stayed by my side...

Thank you God I'm in awe of you
I know who I am and what I must do..believe
You said if you'd be lifted up you'd draw all men unto you..receive
I'm done with the old man now, I'm trusting you....
How about you?

The Concerns of ME

Mrs. Bondar said that this is my best outlet for releasing my true emotions…
so here it goes:

I'm clearly trying to get passed this chapter in my life but it's just not the piece of cake I thought it would be. I've gotta believe it. I've gotta believe it.

It's slightly hard to understand because in my mind it doesn't play out the way it probably should, and that's not good…I over process it; I over process it.

I get disappointed because things never go the way I expect them to or just the way I think they should play out. That hurts me instantaneously because things I don't understand bruise me deeply…I've gotta get a grip…I've gotta get a grip…

See,
I've never had the nicest clothes
The nicest shoes
Biggest house
Or even a car!
So what I don't understand is why so many females hating me like I'm some freaking super star?
Just because I'm the brightest star doesn't mean I'm tryna steal yo' fame
We should be locking together not tryna pull each other down in an attempt to get out of the flame!

Look.
Peep this.
Check this.
Put this in your pipe and smoke it,
Stop tryna put out the light of my heart
Just quit, relax, you're getting ahead of yourself,
  You're choking!

I know, I know, Mrs. Bodnar, if I don't have anything nice say, don't say it, I didn't mean what I said y'all, I was just joking.

Seriously, stop trying to hurt me and keep me down; cause it doesn't hurt anymore it just making me mad. I mean I guess I should be thanking y'all cause y'all unleashed a power in me I never even know I had.

The power to be cut throat just from the words my mouth speaks. The power to intimidate you with my mind, and when you begin to attack, I just turn the other cheek. Because, beauty has nothing to do with my physical appearance or with what your eyes may see. Beauty has everything to do with my knowledge, my experiences; my heart…beauty is with in me.

I am not the academic scholar that I probably should be. I'm sorry, but that's just out how life played out for me. Mrs. Bodnar did say to fully get over something you have to address it completely.

Dad, I may not become a doctor, but I know I have big dreams. It's like your expectations are extremely high and I know you don't mean to add so much pressure but that's how it seems. I know the economy is in bad shape, so I won't go to college and blow all your hard earned money. I'm set on a mission so try and trust me please, even though it might seem a little funny.

To everyone:

Stop hatin'

Stop playin'

Stop over pressuring me.

Because as much as it may hurt, I can't be what everyone wants me to be.

The more you try to change me

The more I become my own adversary

Because, you people are like weeds

You're wrapping yourself around my roots

And suffocating my tree,

I'm so dangerously entangled in the emptiness of all of y'all expectations

I can't even see.

And when I finally come crawling out of the commotion, everyone is satisfied...but me

I'm sorry I had to say it, Mrs. Bodnar,

I just wanna be happy.

I just wanted to tell them, that I can't fulfill all of their destinies

So, now I'm stepping out of this hole...and I'm going to leave...

Because carrying all of this weight will truly kill me

No this life isn't cake but that's cool cause

I need my veggies

I have to love myself,

That's the only way I'll succeed.

I Give

I give my heart
To have and to hold
To love and to cherish
Until we grow old

I gave you my heart
So it might not break
At one point you almost broke it
But you just gave It a little shake

I give you my life
So that we might share
The treasures and memories
That we both care

I gave you my life
That you might show
How it feels to be loved
But you didn't even know

I give you my mind
So we can figure out
This whole love game
And what it's all about

I gave you my mind
So that we could share our thoughts
But our thoughts almost brought on our downfall
And that's both of our faults…

Psalms 56:8

2010

Psalms 56:8

Secret Admirer

My sweet secret admirer
Watches from miles away
Waiting for his moment
For his chance to say

Say what he's been feeling
Say what I didn't know he felt
To utter those heart felt words…
That I'm sure will make me melt

Melt into a puddle
And slip from the grip of his arms
Who is this masked stranger?
With this creative charm

I swear he came from outer space
Someone so beautiful can't be from around here
And he wants to give his heart to me,
And that's what I honestly fear

Fear that I won't be able something that means so much
With the proper delicate care
I tried to tell him about my phobia
He still isn't going anywhere

He says he thinks I'm beautiful
As beautiful as someone can be
I don't know what he's looking at,
Cause that's not at all what I see

Psalms 56:8

I see someone that's been hurt
Someone who's scared to take a chance
Someone who's been hoodwinked
By a little thing called romance

Do you know what he says to me?
He says "baby you're my star,
And I don't care how long it takes for me to get to you
Ill travel any distance, I don't care how far."

"How far I have to walk
How far I have to run
I won't stop until I get you
Cause baby you're the one."
My sweet secret admirer
Who doesn't seem too far away…
We're now living in the moment together
And this is where we'll stay

A True Leader

Doctor King:
"As we walk we must pledge to always march ahead."
President Obama:
"We must become the change we want to see."
Pastor Wright:
"It's not about us, it's about the Lord

It was once stated, the reason that we are where we are today is because our leaders die and the problem stays. The problem stays because we that are still living, won't step up to the plate and direct.
Well, forgive me for pushing it, but, I object.

A leader is someone who guides others to the Lords restoration
A leader is like a shepherd who steers his sheep to a certain destination
A leader is someone who practices what they preach and that takes preparation

A true leader is someone who is equipped in knowing who they are in Jesus Christ.
I don't know about you but to me that's Pastor Wright
That's right, I say you're a true leader is Pastor Wright
For keeping the faith and fighting the good fight

Because honestly you could have easily turned your back and took flight…
But you stayed because God had his flawless hand over your life

And in my close,
We must become the change we want to see, and remember it's all about Jesus and has nothing to do with you and me. You marched ahead and kept the pledge and that's what continues history.

Psalms 56:8

I Can't Fly

There's a crazy difference from the way you
Expect things to go and the way they actually go
You can do your best, proving that you're the ultimate option …
And STILL no one will even come knocking at your door.

Man, being the best means nothing to me anymore.
It's almost impossible when trying to fit
The metal mold of other's outlook on life

How much does it have to shine
For you to understand that it's gold?
Cause I been trying my hardest for years
And honestly this crap is getting old.

Some people just don't see it
I guess some people never will
That's not my fault; I didn't cause the problem
It's not my wound to heal…

I want to be happy, God knows more than anything
But happiness just seems entirely too far off to reach
I cannot be a better person
Will anyone accept me for me?

Do you have any idea how disappointing it is to try
To show someone who just doesn't see it, that you are who you say you are?
Try having almost everyone you encounter be that blind
And not have a your heart turn to stone

Psalms 56:8

How much does it have to shine?
For you to understand that it's a diamond in the ruff?
Well, you snooze, you loose
And living with that will be immensely tough

Some people just don't see it
I guess some people will never try
I gotta let go and move on,
It's weighing me down and I can't fly

My Troubles

Ain't that much talent in the world. I'm TELLING YOU, ain't that much talent in the world, to have everybody constantly, and I mean constantly down my throat trying to tell me
What I can
And cannot do
Or what I'm good enough
Or not good enough
To get done
There just ain't that much jealousy in the world. There ain't to have people
Back stabbing the mess out of me
Viciously attacking me
And expect me not to have the ordasity
To get heated or express my rage too,
Ain't that much competition in the world, there's not. To have them so intimated by me that they have to hawk me down and try to devour my
Confidence
Pride and
Self-worth
There must be something wrong, cause
Ain't that much love in the world, to have them love me sooo much that they
…Completely forget that I exist…

Ugh! See this is what I don't freaking get, how in the world can you really love me and spend your entire life knowing me
And "caring" for me
Because I'm family
And then just up and flip the script?
I'm pissed
I'm an 18 year old woman now so I'm clear up what you remedial,
So called Christians missed.

Don't you dare come up in here and try to repeat the motions of a holy
Christian
And expect that facade to sell
Yo, you a grown behind man,
Standing in front of the church
Encouraging the youth
Sexting
Leading and corrupting the youth
You on a one way ticket to hell!

An another thing, here do you and your people get off with abandoning
your own flesh and blood for a wanna be she-wolf in heat? Oh my bad,
that's your baby right? Get checked for some STD's.

Do you see how disappointment and frustration can make a person's pain
weight a ton?
You see, what you did to me? You don't just do to someone.
It's funny cause now I see you're looking a little unseay,
I bet you wishing this poem was done.
Scribble, scribble tock
Scribble tock
Scribble, hummer
I know my boldness comes as a shock
Well, guess what?
Take a number.
Yeah, I'm speaking my flame,
And I got a lot to say,
So if the truth is a little too hot for you,
The exit is that a way!
Red
Purple
Green
Yellow
Red
Yellow

Yellow
Excuse my rudeness, this is the new reinvented me
HELLO
The more I reinvent myself,
For me and not for others
The more I start to recognize you
And see your true colors

But he'll take those dark colors and make a rainbow, for God is the
ultimate light and that's the light I'll follow
I'm growing and I'm learning but God's still shaping me
I won't be bonded too much longer, because whom the Son sets free is
truly free indeed.
I know you're not listening so I won't talk
I'll let you see.

Wanted

I hate feeling unwanted...I don't understand it...I'm such a want-able person.

I shake a lot...I never understood why...I think it's because I almost never express my anger. I always think of how the other person might feel before I show any emotion other than concern...I shake when I hold in any emotion other than happiness or content.

I hate feeling unwanted. But it's the feeling I'm most familiar.

I sleep a lot. Because that's my only true way of escape...but at the same time, I'm a fearer of anything that's dark...meaning I am deeply afraid of the darkness that surrounds me as I rest. I can't be a peace because I don't know relaxation...unless I'm sleeping during the light hours. I'm afraid of what I can't see because the things I can see want no...no part of me.

I hate feeling unwanted. I don't understand it. I'm such a want-able person...

I'm tired of coming home to me..

I'm tired of rocking myself all the time to sleep...

I wanna breath

I wanna live

I wanna feel my feet....

I wanna love

I want trust...

But no one's giving that to me...

In the toiled twisted thoughts of my mind I travel, and always end up at this broken down rotting tree...

The tree is empty...

Is that why I keep returning here? Is this tree foreshadowing what is to become of me?

In the slow beating trampled island that is my heart...

Psalms 56:8

The water's no longer upon the shore

The tourist no more gather at my steeps… the plants often wonder what they're living for…

What am I living for?

I hate feeling unwanted…but it's the feeling I'm most familiar

Who I am in Christ

Salvation
Dedication
Determination
And separation
Are all a part of your preparation
Of being a true leader for the Lord
Salvation
Cause you got to know who you are in Jesus Christ
When the devil asks you once
Make sure you tell him twice
That you are an heir to the throne
A child of a man that has all might
So you'll take your place on the battle field
And you're not giving up without a fight
Dedication
Is important
Just don't quit
Follow through
Because it's only in God
All your dreams you can pursue
Determination
Is a virtue
Just keep your mind on the prize
Imagine what it would be like
In a world where you'll never have to cry
Jesus is my savior
Jesus in my life
Jesus is my father
And that's who I am in
Jesus Christ

Psalms 56:8

I Am Ready For Love

I'm ready for love
If you'll just give me the chance
I promise my love won't fade
In time my love will only enhance

I'm ready to speak
Those words that will tickle your ear
I promise to say them with meaning
But only if you're willing to hear

I'm ready to learn
What you're willing to teach
I promise to pay close attention
I'll remember every word of your speech

I'm ready to experience
All of the joy and the hurt
I promise I won't give up on us
I'll do anything to make it work

I'm ready for love
I'm ready to care
I'm ready to give up my everything
I'm ready to always be here
I'm ready for love

Free Verse

I understand the test and challenges.
The boldness and lack of fear it takes….to complete such a massive task.
I am a conqueror.
I am a hero.
I am change.
I've felt the animosity of thousands of enemies…
I've stared in the face of danger.
I stood my ground unmovable, unshakeable;
in order to get my people free.
I am a conqueror
I am a hero.
I am change.
I know what it means to have courage.
I do not ask about the trials he's faced.
I don't ponder his journey.
I myself becomes him.
I am a conqueror.
I am a hero.
I am President Barrack Obama.

Psalms 56:8

Freedom

Freedom
Let freedom ring.
The oppressed cannot remain repressed forever…
And the tough times won't seem so rough…
If we just stick together
Just
Unjust
Why is it that we can get away with breaking some rules?
While being forced to obey others?
Why is it that the penalty is way worse on a black man
Who kills some one of the white race than
it is if he kills his own brother?
The fact that you are a black man
Living at a tip toe stance
You'd never know your full potential
Cause society would never give you the chance.
At a time when no one knew of the word integrity,
Along came Doctor Martin Luther King Jr. who said:
"As we walk, we must pledge to always march a head"
Dr. King said: "We, Cannot, turn back!"
For this reason and this reason only
Black history could never be dead.
Because Dr. King followed the morals of his four fathers,
He's now waiting for us at home.
That's why we should stand up for what's right,
Even if we're standing alone
POWER

2011

Psalms 56:8

I am Love

I remember it being something like golden…yeah, I remember it as golden.
I remember smelling nature at its perfection, the flowers, the grass, the trees…the wind
Sweet smelling beauty…sweet smelling serene

Oh, I remember the feeling; feeling like nothing or no one could bring me down from the cotton laced clouds that I called home…
The touch was smooth, I remember the touch and it was so gentle that if I pressed too hard, like and egg I tell you; like an egg it would crack into a thousand and one pieces…a thousand and one irreplaceable pieces…

Love you see, I do remember
I remember love in a thousand and one different ways

I remember it being a down poor…
A down poor of uncontrollable emotions…I don't want to remember but I remember the chill of that down poor as each emotion, like ice drops, damaged my skin…I remember the inner body damage.

In the long drawn out days that are my past I've learned
I've learned to be who I am and trust in who I am to make it. I am love, love is within me.

This is to you, as I write…
I write with you in mind; with you in heart
Because my pain will no longer bring you pleasure…
I've been freed…I am a butterfly

Psalms 56:8

I walked away in fear, but now I will stroll with dignity; with pride
I will travel down this rocky road with thoughts of a soft surface.
I will keep my head held high
I am love and I remember me.

To you who said I wouldn't live
Here I am…and I'm breathing,
Breathing breaths of confidence in the belief that my life's purpose is bigger
than just me…
I am whole
I am love
And I am Complete

Not a Goodbye But, I'll See you Later

The words that I never wanted to say about you...
Are now the only words that facts will speak.
I've never even fathomed the fact that I'd ever have the opportunity to mumble..
"You were" "You would have been.." "Rest in peace.."
It was said your final thoughts were that your situation is "win, win",
If you lived to see another day, you'd win.
But if you slept... only to be awakened by the Lord Jesus Christ himself, you'd also win.
The only proper response to that my dear pastor is AMEN.

Amen to your purpose, your destiny and how loud the message of your life roared.
You said it was never about you; you said it was always about the Lord...
Dear God you took your time with his creation. Heavenly father you couldn't have been more precise.
Because even in his death, Pastor Wright modeled life.

Lord prepare me, to be a sanctuary, pure and holy, tried and true...
Your lessons will give me growth, Positivity, honor and I will forever share with whom ever I encounter my memories of you.

You too have finished your race a fought the good fight...Thank you for your patience,
This is not a goodbye but more like a see you later father Wright..

Psalms 56:8

1 Shot + Message = ME

What is this? This world that we call home today,
Is it truly our home or is it a prison in the middle of a demon's masquerade?
Twinkle, twinkle, twinkle, justice is too far off to see…we're letting death
overpower life….& that's just not what I'm going to accept it to be.

1 Shot + 1 Message =ME

The shot: the shot that paralyzed the faith of a whole community; the shot
that just doesn't seem to come with a sense of peace. The shot that shook
the community and brought us crashing down to our knees… the shot
that came with meaning and until it's discovered…will not cease. Now
that we're broken, what's next?

The message: the message that one person truly makes a difference…the
messages says even angels die too. The message is that he finished his race
and completed his destiny and that the only one missing the message is
you! The message is that tomorrow is not promised; to be honest neither
is the end of today. You've got to get yourself together; live right for your
time is speeding away. Ok, that's a good message, but what does it equal?

It equals Ahman B. Fralin
It equals the amazing lessons his presences taught
His mortal life was cut short in his innocents…but he still wouldn't call
anyone's faults
It equals the ultimate role model,
The a real definition of forgiveness and love
Love= Ahman B. Fralin
Ahman B. Fralin demonstrated love

So it doesn't matter the criminal world we live in
Because this twisted life isn't for me
I got the message Ahman sent us
1 shot + 1 message = me!

Did You?

I can say you used me, I hate you
I miss you, how could you? Until I'm blue
In the face
But what will that solve or change?
They're just words; Just feelings ...
The memories will leave their trace... (I wish you well)

I wanted things to be different
Because this feeling I'm feeling, I don't like
But I cannot explain
I bit off more than I could chew
Now I'm barely taking the pain...
I could never admit anything
Because my pride would be too ashamed
We were in this together so I refuse to carry the blame
You make me look bad; you'd have to take my last name
I'm above my own expectations
& you just won't let me go
Now that I came

& I think you expected me to respond
In a completely different way
Did you think I would be eating out the palm of your hand?
Did you? Did you think I'd be submissive?
Submissive like a dog?
Passive like a dog?
Oh, Stupid, like a dog.
Not then, not now, not ever.

& You know what? If we were going to play this pet game
I'd definitely be the owner
Because I trump you superiorly
I'd be the dominatrix, you'd be the moaner.
Whoa.

2012

Find Peace

The world doesn't love itself
Therefore the world can love nobody
Death doesn't fear itself
Therefore death takes ANYBODY
Anton Cofield
Jonathan Kotz
Ahman Fralin
Hasan Hayes…
Treyvon Martin
Michael Dunn
This is written specifically in your light
Those silent voices that rant loudly in the night
Speak up! Speak Loud! Tell us what is your fight?
Stop! They're saying, this is not the way to find peace!
Rioting, reverse racism, the hatred must all cease!
While we're resting, let us rest, it's temporary, let us sleep.
Justice will take place, and the ultimate authority will reign
There's life after death and those who murdered us will experience inconsolable pain…
Stay sane…friends…my family count this as a gain…
I've lived, I've dreamed…fulfilled my destiny..don't give me fame
The world doesn't love itself, listen to me,
So the world will never love anyone else….
Let's turn our anger into strength, stand together
And help others through what we've felt
Life is cold, but death is even colder,
While you still have each other cherish that moment
Because death is only getting bolder

Psalms 56:8

To The Boy Who Had Me

(Bottom Stanza's written to the song Doo Wop
(That Thing) By Lauryn Hill)

Both: To the boy who had me

(B)1: I love you   **2:** I hate you

1: You make me feel so good. Like all the work I put into doing my hair and this skirt I hiked up didn't go unnoticed. You make me feel worth something.

2: I feel as though I have nothing to offer, so what's there for you to gain? Feeding me sweet nothings and filling my head with empty dreams…I don't wanna be your mattress…

B: Even if it is for just one night.

1: I love the rush you give me
Your lips, my lips
Where we place our finger tips
The hiding the seeking
The moaning the screaming
I'm not looking for Mr.Right…more like…Mr. All night

2: I remember that night
"don't take your panties off…just pull them to the side"
Just let me slide, you want this, stop being shy…
So I did…and that's when my self-esteem died.

B:1.I want on your ecstasy ride 2.I want off your ecstasy ride

1:love ain't got nothing on sex
2:sex ain't better than love

(Both at same time)
1.   Cause when you're going, I'm going and it really gets hot
& I'm willing to scream like you just hit my spot! I know by giving it to
you my chances will pop, I'll move up on your list, maybe hit the top.
"Oh my God!"
I love you

2. Cause when we started I was scared I wanted you to stop
but you were grabbing and panting and you were on top, I'm laying
here it's my fault, I will never be a cop
your regard for me dropped....

(Gasps)

2.It's been three weeks since you been looking for your friend....
1.The one you let hit & never called you again...
2. Was it even worth it if you had to pretend
1. If you didn't want to why you lay down with him
Both: Baby girl.
1. You are the flower
Both: Sunshine
2. You deserve equal power
Both: Honey Bun
1.You don't have to fabricate
Both: Sacred one
2. It's you that creates

1: in everything I believed to be beautiful...
2:It's happened to all of us
1: in all that I feel...
2: Waiting for our seat on the love bus
1: I can't love,
2: YES YOU CAN
1:I'm cold hearted
2: LOVE YOURSELF
1: They're all selfish
1&2: all men seem the same to me...
1: But How?
2: Find your purpose
1: & then what?
2: Believe, really believe you're worth it
Both: Just cause it is, doesn't mean it has to be.

1: If I decide not to hook up any more. & say this game is no longer for me
How will I get a man to love me?
What will my worth be?

2: We lost sight of it but we're queens.
& if I gotta give everything i possess to man that ain't my husband, the boy is not for me .We are not sexual objects, we are human beings

Both: we just wanna be seen

1: and not just as women though
2: I need to be seen as a person
1: I need to be seen as
Both: ME

2013

Psalms 56:8

Captivate

Can I captivate you?

Show you me?

Who I can really be? I can be everything you need...

Can I captivate you?

Send you on a ride, a fantasy trance that travels inside, my imagination, your fixations, true sensations, of my dreams...of me and you. Baby,

Can I captivate you?

Now I'm your regular round the way girl, not much sex appeal, not much class.

It's just something about you,

That makes me wanna plump up my ass, when you walk pass, me.

My emotions crash, thrash, mash... I want you to be, mines

I don't know maybe in time, you'll drown in my rhyme, I'll place you under a spell, boy, I won't tell, your secrets.

Let me into your heart & I'll keep it.

You won't know unless you try,

Let me captivate you with my eyes, my thighs, my smile. Let me sedate you with my style, I promise I'll drive you wild...baby trust me. Let me captivate you.

Psalms 56:8

Notice Me

Who can I be?
In a loveless world we call home....
Where can I be free?
To be what I want and not be crucified for such.....
For such, acceptance...
When I lay my head down at night,
It's in fright because I'm still going.
Still searching, hoping, wanting,
You to want me, entirely
Please, this is me...
No definite answer of beauty
No solid evidence that I'm unique
I'm incomplete.
I'm not pretty enough for you to see,
I not strong enough for you to see
I'm not "you" enough for you to see
I'm not smart enough, I'm not fun enough...
But I want you. I dream of you...
I deserve you...but you don't notice me.

2014

Ugly

A knock at the door, I answer
But no one has come for me
I don't know why it's so hard for me to believe
That I am ugly
Overlooked and often gone unseen,
When you see me you don't even tell me
I guess that's because you too also believe…
That I am…
Hold my hand
I don't wanna view the scenes
Of me so desperately
Wanting for you…to just once see me
Notice me
Believe me when I share my beauty….
I can't help that I am ugly….

Psalms 56:8

Imagery

You didn't really want to come…
Why didn't you just tell me so?
I'm waiting for you
I'm wanting for you…
Desperate for you…
Time is so impossible…I stare at the clock, then at the door, back at the clock, over and over love…
But not a minute has passed.
That embrace…warm snug embrace, wrapping me tight in your breath taking cocoon, indulging me in a trance and, I just, I just feel free.
Please help me…because I know that we could never be, more than a vision Of toxic…IMAGERY
Forever, my God, what happened to our forever?
Time is so impossible.
Every face that passes,
Every footstep I hear,
Every fragrance I smell, I think of you.
I'm drowning, heart beating, I'm bleeding you.
Let go I tell myself, if it's meant to be, It'll be…
But did Juliet let go of Romeo?
Did Rose sink Jack?
Did Noah stop believing in Ally?
I know, there all just fantasies.
I gotta step into reality
And maybe start believing in me…
I just wish I knew,
When that day will be…
Until then, I'm just a piece…
Just a fragment of me…
A prisoner, of IMAGERY…

My Haters Taught Me that

I mean everybody loves you
When you have something that they want
When they can see the success you'll bring them
When they see how much you stunt.

But ain't nobody got nothing for you
When you need a hand to hold
A caring touch on touch on the back
A blanket, a warm meal to ease your soul

Nothing. Not a got damn thing.
Yet they throw you in front of an audience
In front of a crowd "sing baby sing"
"You make me so proud"
But when we're alone it's that
I'm to dramatic; I'm talking to loud
Then Freaking listen
Your perception of me rises and ends on what you
Think other people think of me…
Can you see?
And I still look to you for confirmation
That's what I can't believe
That's where the self-hate manifest, man
That's where it breeds.

I don't wanna…I don't wa…I'm tired
Of saying what I don't want to do.
I cannot continue to make everyone happy.
I'm out growing these freaking shoes…

Psalms 56:8

I wanna live so I guess there are just something's
I gotta let go
Maybe I won't be one of the greatest writers…
Maybe you'll never love me
Maybe I'll never see my worth
Maybe…I'll never sell out a show…
It's the future man,
I really don't know

But what I do know,
That I know that I know,
That you need to know,
That the world should know
That it knows that it knows…
Something's gotta give.

I wanna live
I will live
I gotta live
Cause no one's gonna appreciate me like I can
No one's gonna love me here on this earth and fulfill my life's span
No one's gonna say, "dang girl, you look beautiful" even when I'm in my
sweat pants…
And ya'll taught me that
In this society, everybody wants recognition
"Oh Serena, remember when I…."
Nah, I'll pat my own back
I don't want to be my worst enemy
Everybody does a great job with that
You only get one shot, and while I'm here
I won't crack.
My haters taught me that.

Psalms 56:8

I Wanna' be Free

I wish I would write more,
There are so many emotions bottled up inside me…
I wish I had someone to love me,
There's so much love pouring out of me.
I wanna be free.
Like the wind in the trees,
Like the stars placed so beautifully,
Above the skyline of New York City…
Like everything I've ever wanted…
Everything just beyond my reach.
Teach me,
I wanna be,
What you call beauty…
I wanna be your specialty.
Don't take part please,
Take all of me…take all of me.
There's so much confusion building up around me, drowning me.
I don't know who you want me to be…
I wish I could talk more,
There's so much to get out of me.
I wish I would do more…
There's so much of this amazing world I haven't seen…
Hold me.
So tight…make me see
That I'm worth the opportunity,
That there's a place for me …
That you believe in me,
That you want me…

Psalms 56:8

Too Many Reasons

There will never be another man like you
No such patience and warmth like you
So gentle, perfection in all that you do
Too many reasons to love you

I remember it like it was yesterday….
Winter's chill took over the earth…
Spring so far away…
It was for me your valentine
$1.35, and a flower,
Let me remind you if I may…
You said, this is all I have but I'll work and be back in a little while,
I'll make a way…
That moment my heart was yours,
I had never been anybody's and you took my breath away…
There will never be another man like you,
No such patience and warmth like you…
Too many reasons to love you

You hadn't known me for that long,
Yet it feels like you were there for every call
Nurturing me with lessons in laughter, helping to cover my scars,
Like the time we were delivering newspapers,
You remember, the dog was chasing us all
I crack up thinking of you running like that,
Would have thought you were escaping the law.
There will never be another man like you
So gentle, perfection in all that you do
Too many reasons to love you

Psalms 56:8

You had always given us what we needed
You tried your best to give us what we wanted as well,
Did you forget changing the tags on my coat,
So we could get a better sell?
Just these minor things I value
Oh, and I promise I won't tell because,
There will never be another man like you,
No such patience and warmth like you,
Daddy, there so many reasons to love you…
You've known us forever…
Crowded together on your pull out bed
Waiting outside of aunt Daisy's for you to meet the ice cream truck
The fantasies you piled into our heads…Thank you,
Enough cannot be said, you see
There will never be another man like you
No such patience and warmth exist like you
So sweet and gentle, perfection in all that you do
Way too many reasons to love you…

Hey You

Hey you,
Sometimes I randomly think of you and the
Possibilities of what could have been…
I think to myself in these moments,
"What was I missing back then?
What did I not see?
So much time has passed now
You probably don't even remember me…
I've experienced others since us and
It's become evident that you were truly rare.
I didn't care,
I was so naively willing to share…
You.
Of course now, I wouldn't dare to
Do the things I impulsively did do
During the times I should have valued you.
Listen, I was young, we were young
And I just wanted to be cool
Cheesy, I know.
My god, you're so cute…
I'm secretly admiring you
If you were able to get this message,
Would you feel it too?
Would you know I was talking only to you?
Would your heart skip a beat, like mine
Does when I see a picture of you?
I hope so,
If you feel it,
I'm waiting for you
Make a move.
XO, SNC

Escape

I guess I should just,
Shush up this crying and…wipe my face
After years of fighting for you, protecting you,
And loving you…
I still don't feel safe.
And. Looking at where we are now, I guess I'm still
Easy…to replace.
So here I am, with my pen and my notebook
Ready to escape
Free my mind for a little while,
Drown in outer space.
I'm so tired of being invested in someone who
Wouldn't take my place
Done trying to be a stain anymore
I quit trying to be something you can't erase
I am though. You won't admit it but
You're the flower…
I'm the vase.
But that's still not enough
So here, here's the last of me
And I hope you enjoy my taste…
As you swallow remember
Now is just a little too late
Bet loving me now doesn't seem like such a waste
No. I'll let myself out
I'm closing this gate
No more control
I'm the master of my fate
Ready to escape.

Psalms 56:8

2015

I Hope You Hear

I don't know what it is
That makes us as humans
Do the things we do.
Maybe we're searching for something
For that "Yes I like you too" from our crush that we never got
For that promise our moms and pops made us
But never followed through
…I guess they forgot
When somebody like me dies,
Yea they make T-shirts
Hold candle light vigils
Stand in circles united and tell stories about
How I made them feel…
But never being fully honest
Not at all keeping it real
Forgetting that it was me,
Pushing drugs through our streets
In the dead of night
Conveniently forgetting that I was me,
Jumping the young boys on the block
And selling their bikes
Listen, I'm not saying I don't deserve to be remembered and loved
 It's just death has no age limit
And selfishness is its drug
I just want the boys in the younger generation to learn from what I did
Trust me when I tell you
This murderous lifestyle is no way to live.

Psalms 56:8

Teach them of my short comings
Expose them to my flaws
Unlock the mental chains of social media
Open their ears to the higher call
I just want our men to have it all
Blindness is worse than ignorance
It worse than fear
Our future black men deserve a chance man
I hope you hear.

BENT

So, my co-worker comes up to me at work the other day and says
"You still get excited over Martin Luther King day? I mean isn't his message a little spent?"
I replied, "Change does not role in on the wheels of inevitability, but comes through the continuous struggle. And so we must straighten our backs and work for our freedom. A man can't ride you unless your back is bent." -MLK
Isn't his message a little spent...
I don't know, has social media started paying your rent?
Has Michael Jordan reimbursed you for the bill money you spent?
You brag about how fleeked out you are but get mad when see the word nigga
Cause that part of black you just can't admit,
You scream behind your computers that black lives matter
But are not fully willing, nor ready to commit.
Talking is not enough, your actions have to be president.
Unconsciously you are insinuating that our fight is dead or is that not what you meant?
Somebody please let me vent.
We make Facebook statuses, with our omniscient opinions but
They held a Hands Up, Don't Shoot rally in Philadelphia a few months ago,
How many of y'all went?
"The man can't ride you unless your back is bent."
Excuse me, um, I would like to name just a few things that have us bent:
Black on black crime
Bent
Free my nigga so and so who killed 7 people but he innocent he was just trying to pay his rent
Bent
The overrated obsession with money
Bent

Psalms 56:8

The "I don't need an education as long as I look good phase".
Bent
Cyber bullying
Light skinned vs Dark skins
Over sexualized America
Bent
Listen my brothers and my sisters
This deadweight truly does have us bent
If you think you're winning right now
Think again
Change does not roll in on the wheels of inevitability,
Meaning racism and inequality won't get better by just letting it be
Every day is a continuous fight
And education is the key
Plant it deep down inside you like a seed
Nourish it with love let it flourish
And what you breed
These words can't be more powerful more loud
The whisper "I can't breathe"
Come on family, march with me.

You Bring Out the Art in Me

You couldn't possible see the potential in me baby…
Or else you'd be lying here next to me,
Holding me,
Connecting so deeply,
Creating a masterpiece…
Baby, you bring out the art in me.
Your sun kissed skin
Brown like honey wheat
Voice sent from the heavens
Calmness of the seas
Damn it, you bring out the freak in me
If you'd have me I could show you
Oh, baby, I'd let you see
All the places on my body
Where these other men weren't blessed enough to be
I'd only mist for you and
You'd only swim for me and
We could allow our love to manifest in each stroke; with each beat
Daddy,
Baby,
Honey, love me.
You couldn't possibly see
The potential in me
You act as if you only half-ass want me
But, sugar you're so blind
And God, you're so silly
Yet you bring out the lust in me
The love in me
The hate in me
The peace in me
You bring out the art in me…

Psalms 56:8

I'm The Shit

I know, I know baby…
I'm the shit.
That's why you standing there,
Tongue out
Tail flailing in the air.
You just starting taking another girl seriously? How?
Did you have time to spare?
Cause you're here, but where is she?
I'm the only woman in competition with me.
Cause daddy, I'm. The. Shit.
No ifs, ands, or butts,
No pun intended
But, I warned you of this.
The minute your eyes locked with mines
You knew you'd need another hit.
And now you walk away like you weren't
Hooked on it
Hooked on me,
You traveled out of your way
And never even touched me
But you came back….
Because we made an emotional connection
And that a fact,
Here's another fact
I'm the shit.
How dare you come for me acting so bogus?
Saying I don't know if you'll be cool with this
With what? Competing for you?
Honey I'm a beta fish.

Psalms 56:8

Can't no one else fit in this bowl
I fill the whole dish.
Mhhmm Cause I'm the shit.
And to think I shed some tears over it.
Over thinking you could be the perfect fit
Thinking whatever I lack,
She must have it.
Nah, no, no, I'm. The. Shit
& I'm sure she is too
We as women need to get a grip.
Let these men run wild
And putting up with it.
Cause I was waiting for you at the door,
And when you opened your mouth
I whispered say no more.
Cause I'm the shit
And I know you'll never get over it.

I Was There From the Start

Shit I'm tired of Saying:
"This is what really happened"
"Believe me"
"I'm not WEAK"
"What I do? They coming?"
"Who sent for me?"
Fuck it.
If they coming, tellem' I said come on.
I'M READY.
Standing on the battlefield; War deep
With vengeance in my eyes…
Thoughts of those nights I cried for me…
Those nights I wanted to die…
Screw you.
For making me believe I was weak when I wasn't
For making me think I wasn't worth your loving.
I'm better than you.
I said screw you.
Now you got me out of character
Doing shit I don't even fucking do.
You make me sick,
Got me cussing, drinking, lonely, angry…dark…
I said screw you.
What the freak did I do to you?
What the freak did I…I was there from the start.

Psalms 56:8

My heart…
My heart can't take no more pain…I was there from the start.
Love me.
Why won't you please…can you just love me?
What the fuck mom, I'm sick, "Friends". "Family". I'm sick of this shit…
I was there from the start…
I was there from the start…

Empty

Is it empty?
Or is it just me?
Could it be the way, that I perceive reality?
I don't know, it feels pretty empty to me.
It's the back and forth and back and forth, this thing….
Am I ugly?
Am I good enough?
Am I misunderstood?
Do I have nothing or everything?
Life is bad, life is good….
How does one find value in themselves,
To push through the hard times?
Is it deep down inside?
Is it lost in these rhymes?
Validation in myself; I'm vain
Validation from others; I'm insecure
So which one is it?
Cause I'm not sure
The only thing I am sure of is, the world gives it; support
Then the world takes it away; abort
So what is it?
To cause the world to turn her cold lonely shoulder against me?
I too am of a lonely spirit…I too am of a lonely spirit.
Then I learn I'm not alone…
this lonely spirit has others to connect to.
They lift me up; tell me I'm worth it
That I'm worth everything.

She Has Been Freed

I cannot reach the standards you have set for me
The pressure of trying to figure out your love is…killing me
I don't want to let go
But I'm letting go
You're leaving no other choice for me…
I to, have dreams that I can no longer allow to be imaginary,
What is it that you believe?
That without you,
There'd be no me?
Allow me to show you the reality
I wanted you.
I wanted your acceptance so deeply that I created a need.
I thought that if you thought I needed you,
You'd take the time to get to know me
Then you'd see
That I'm not perfect
But was created so beautifully
…That in my own way I am a masterpiece
I knew if you saw that, you'd really love me
& not just love me because it's your responsibility…
The kind of love that has no distance in between
The kind where you'd see me as evergreen
The kind of love that fills you up and floods you with peace
You feel me?
But instead you saw me as weak
Disgusted; Even at the thought of me
Going through the motions, pretending;
But never really connecting to me…
Those actions branded me
Branded me with insecure feelings, self-hatred and low self-esteem…

Psalms 56:8

My attachment to you became unhealthy
With the love of God
I just wanted you to see me!!
& not to strip me
But to experience me
Your child, mommy…
You hurt me.
Your unrealistic perception
Became my burden to carry
I loved you so much…
Even more than me…
But now it's time for you to take the back seat
I'd even like to take a moment
To re-introduce you to me
Hello my name is Serena Nicole Chapman, the visionary
The girl who was lost in darkness, but can now see
The girl with as many spots a leopard…but is still a masterpiece
Serena Chapman created so beautifully
Serena the " you now have no choice but to see me"
Serena Nicole released from her prison
Because she finally realized she held the key
To her destiny
She has been freed
Now walk in Liberty
She has been freed
She has been set free.

A Rise in Me

You're trying to get a rise out of me
Insulting my intelligence
Pissing me off
You're trying to get a rise out of me.
I must warn you though
With me, you don't want beef
I'll take that pride and hang it
Right from a tree
Psychoanalyze your mannerisms
And diagnose you as weak
Cut you below the belt
You'll have to sit when you pee
Front to back bitch, wipe front to back.
You're trying to bring a rise out of me
I'll sip on your excuses like I sip my tea,
Sugar, you so sweet
I'll make you eat your words like a Christmas feast
Leave your opinion by the door
Where I dry my feet
With me, you don't want beef.
"So it's like that huh? Alright"
Yea buddy it's just like that
Pack your shit and get in line with my other haters
All of y'all whack.
Tryna keep up with my fire, my mind
Might give you an asthma attack
Just breathe
You'll wake up tomorrow with marks and bruises
Cause I beat. That. Ass.

Psalms 56:8

You're trying to get a rise out of me
& if you want it buddy,
I'll give you what you need
I'll release a fury that hell it's self has never seen
Words so mean
Bring you down to your knees
"Stop it Serena ! Please baby, please!!"
You're trying to get a rise out of me
With me you don't want beef
Quit trying to bring a rise out of me
Don't unleash this beast.

BETTER
(Written to the song "Better" By Jessica Reedy)

I was lost
Tried to block out my haters but
But only blocked you from me
"A heart with no beat, a singer with no song to sing"
A dreamer with no vision,
All I saw was who hurt me, they hurt me, I hurt me, You…Hurt…Me
"So I know the feeling, the silence is deafening"
I didn't see
Who I could be
Wrecking my mind
Screaming now can you see me?
"But in the pain lies a blessing"
Now can you see me?
"A sweeter sound victory"
A prisoner trapped in me
"So keep walking and walking and walking"
But what do I have to bring ?
"Keep walking and walking and walking"
I only have this shame…
"Keep walking and walking and walking"
What if they make fun of me.
"So keep walking and walking and walking"
But God, who would believe?
"Though it seems so far"
That you would chose me
"No matter who you are"
To bring you glory
"There's one thing that I know"

Psalms 56:8

You don't want me, Lord
I sin as much as I brush my teeth
I stand up to do your will and they'll laugh at me
"Listen to me, I know you scared your hearts' bleeding"
I'm not worthy God, please don't send me
"What are you going to do now? I think it's time you break free"
From self-doubt?
"I think it's time you break free"
From depression?
"I think it's time you break free"
From the pains of my past? But God, they hurt me
"Free"
Suicide?
"Free"
Fear?
"Free, free, life it can leave you so bitter, bitter, bitter, bitter"
"But you must believe, that it get better, better, better, better"
There's more to the pain
"It's alright, dry your eyes"
Jesus is to gain
"Send a prayer"
Lift up ye hands
"To the sky"
Be ye lifted up, ancient doors
"I know it's hard to fight"
The King of Glory
"But you must believe"
Shall come in
"That it gets better"
For God so loved the world
"So keep walking and walking and walking"

Psalms 56:8

That he gave his only begotten Son"
"Though it seems so far"
That who so ever believeth in him
"No it doesn't really matter who you are"
Shall not perish
"There's one thing that I know"
But have everlasting life
Life it can leave you so bitter
But you must believe that it gets better

Anybody

I'm glad to see you're doing well
We both know why I have no parts of that…
The destruction you caused on that night, what you did…
How could I stay around that?
I thought we had it like that
We were tight like that
Close like that…
Can't get that back
That night I came to you and told you
That I had nobody
That didn't mean touch my body
I'm not just anybody
Can't wash it off my body
Feeling like anybody
I'm not just anybody
I hate watching you grow
Knowing that I can't be a part of that
Remembering how you stole that
When I thought we had it like that
Close like that
Damn, I miss that
Guess I gotta get over that
Cause I'm not just anybody
I'm not just anybody

The Pride You held on too

One day you'll wake up
& that's when you'll see
That the pride you held on to
Wasn't worth losing me
The wind beneath your wings
The potential wife to be
So sad the day you wake up
& your pride has vanished me
I didn't want to leave
Because I thought you were the key
To unlocking the beauty of love
That was hidden in me
"I wanted to reach out days ago"
You whispered
"But my pride wouldn't let it be"
You cannot have
What you are not willing to fight to keep
I hope you wake up
Your pride is not worth losing me
"The old me wouldn't have chased you"
You said
"The old me would have let you leave"
"But when I went to run after you, the new me wouldn't move my feet"
Well tell the old you that the new you needs to set you free
Because the new you is what's going to have the old you
Waking up lonely

Psalms 56:8

Listen, I don't know who hurt you
I just know it wasn't me
The alarm is going off wake up!
Your pride is strangling me
One day you'll wake up
& I hope it's not too late to see
That the pride that you held onto
Wasn't worth losing me.

Midnight Concubine

I could show you a good time
I could deprive you of your time
I could spin all the way around
Make my waist do the whine
Up & down, round & round
Make your spirits rise
I like to devour my men.
After one night I'm usually done.
X marks the spot
Checked off
Hole In one.
Oh and don't try to contact me
No texts
Unless it's 911, hit me
Then I'll show up in your door way
Handle that emergency, I'll give you what you want.
Don't go crying for me.
You know the rules now play your part
Grab me kiss me, please me,
But you're off limits to my heart.
Don't pretend
You don't care
I'm an item in your shopping cart
She icy, she cold
But what made me that way?
Your love in the heat of the night
Then your absolute absence during the day
How many times does a girl have to be thrown away
Before she begins to play?

Psalms 56:8

Like I said papi,
I can show you a good time
Elegant, and mysterious
But no good intentions in mind
Midnight concubine

I Can't Stay

I must have played it over a thousand times
Thought about it over and over
Contemplated losing my mind
You see,
I don't get how you can give somebody
Everything you have; Do your very best
Every day
And they'll still want to leave
They wanna leave you
They don't believe in you
Yet, they tell you lies
They bottle your cries
Cause they don't know what they want
They sample other pies
See, you can't be too good to an entitled person
They think with minimum effort they deserve the prize
Cause you talk about the "We"
And they respond with "I"
"I've been through too many bad relationships"
"I'm not letting that happen this time"
"I'm too old to play these games"
Yet everything that comes out their mouth is a rhyme
I connected to you
Cause I see something in you
That's why it's not easy to walk away
But you don't see it in yourself
And you're not even trying

Psalms 56:8

That's why I can't stay
I can't stay
I Cannot stay
Serena, you're too beautiful
Just walk away
If it's meant to be it'll flourish
If not, it's natural to decay
Either way you're worth more
So remember
That's why you can't stay.

To The Boy in the Corner

Here's a little tale about a boy who
Would retreat to his dark little corner
When he didn't know what to do
He watched his mother experience
Countless amounts of abuse
Yet, he was forced to watch in silence
Filled with fear he felt he was no use
"look at me" he thought
"They even make fun of me at school"
Curly hair, thin body & old dirty shoes
" I'll stay here in this corner
Until it's safe that's what I'll do"
"Daddy..." The boy called
"Can I just sit right here with you?
Everything's changing, I'm growing up
& I don't have a clue"
"When a girl tells me she loves me,
Should I love her too?
Wait, is love something you say?
Dad or is it something you do"
The boy's father didn't answer
Just because a fathers there
Doesn't mean he's present too.
The little boy became so confused
So he retreated back to his little corner
He didn't know what else to do
His nights became colder
You better believe lonelier too
Because even though relationships came
They went,
His pride became the issue

Psalms 56:8

"I've been hurt; no one's really down,
Screw the old me, I'm about to get new"
He began to expect everything
Yet always deep down believing he was of no use
Entitlement, darkness, and misery
A dangerous combination you see
He walked around wanting to give love, but not knowing how to accept
love
He ended up empty
Wanting to end his life
Empty
Holy matrimony to misery
Empty
Self-destructing
Emptiness
Completing his own self-fulfilling prophecy
"I'm not worth it, I'll stay in this corner,"
"Nobody will really love me "
Boy in the corner
With your streaming tears
That no one helped you dry
How long will you accept no one?
How long will you be the root of your own demise?
If you don't put in the work to fix it
The way you are is the way you'll die
Boy in the corner
Won't you come out?
There's no more need to hide
Step out little boy and see
That time is passing you by.

Like That

Why won't you just pick up the phone and call me please?
Why you gotta act like that?
Let your pride sabotage like that?
Ruin our love like that?
You act like you get to mess up and I gotta apologize
Like I made you cry
Like I kept you up all night, man,
Why you gotta act like that?
Let you pride win like that
Ruin our love like that?
Remember that day you told me I was worth it?
Then you disappeared
Like you didn't hear
Yourself speaking
I came to you without seeking
And even with that you weren't keeping
Me
Why you gotta act like that?
Let your past get the best of you like that
Self-fulfilling prophesied like that?
It ain't even gotta be like that.
Now you gotta miss out
Now you'll search for me in all your loves
And I will not be found
Cause my love was profound
More than just a sound
I was a song
And you'll remember me always
& wish for the old days

Psalms 56:8

But I will not be found
Someone else will take your crown
All because you wouldn't speak up,
Cause you chose to act like that
Let your pride run like that
Let it take something you can't get back
Just like that

Down On Me

When the rain is coming down
When the ocean's at ease
When the leaves flow through the sky like feathers
You are pleasing to me
Skin so sweet its decadent
Kisses taste like peppermint
Pecan tan, a golden tint
Ink trials decoding your body
It's your blueprint
When the rain is coming down
When the ocean's at peace
When the leaves flow through the sky like feathers
You are inside of me
Strong and confident
You guide me
Gentle yet so much power
I scream
Tight like my best dress
You fit me
Deep Inside of me
Driving me crazy
When the rain is coming down
You're down on me
When the ocean's at ease
You are one with me
When the leaves flow through the sky like feathers
You are releasing me
Rain down on me
Ocean at ease
Feather filled trees
You are setting me free

Psalms 56:8

I Was Falling in Love With You

What are you trying to do to me?
Hurt me like the world has hurt you?
I. Am. Not. Them.
I was falling in love with you.
You really thought I was joking didn't you
When I said I didn't fully understand love
Couldn't comprehend how someone could really give me love
How could you love me and not want to hurt me
But if you hurt me you can't love me
Yet if you don't hurt me it can't be love
I don't know and I don't get it.
Am I not worthy of?
Dammit, baby why?
Why? Can you just tell me why?
You forced me to open up and let you in
Shit, I. Tried.
You left me though
No matter how I cried.
I told you I was not her.
I proved that I would ride
You shut down any way.
Damn you & your pride.
I was falling in love with you.
I was falling in love with you
My days were eternal
The days that I spent with you
You didn't want me though
How could you just walk away?
You don't even try.

Psalms 56:8

2016

Psalms 56:8

Lost Yo Mind?

Have you lost your mother fucking mind?
Thinking you can ease your way back in
Ease yourself back into wasting my time?
You tried it.
Missed me with the bullshit
I dodged it.
Gave you full access to my treasure
You robed it
Talking about "I truly do miss you"
Boy bite it.
Coming back around with no apology.
Don't bet on that astrology
I'll show you something the stars did not see
Cause this time you pissed off all of me.
And I was answers
It better be HIV
Lung disease
Boy, it better be cancer
I mean your reasons better be legit
Opening me up like that to just quit
Man screw all this.
This isn't even me, you made me like this
Carving deeper into my wound
It's now a bottomless pit
Got me cussing you out & cursing your next trick
There's no way I deserved this
& here you come
Head so far up your ass all I see is chest
Talking about "I'm just checking on you"

Psalms 56:8

Like that's gonna pass the test
Thank you sir, I'm fine
Take a lap, dust off and try one more time
Cause you must have lost your mother fuckingg mind.
To think such little effort could fly.
Come correct or not at all.
Boy bye…

You're No Good For Me

I know you're not good for me.
Maybe that's why I hold on to you
Cause you didn't want me.
Maybe I wouldn't want me either.
I don't know.
I just know I tried.
I gave you what I had.
I cried.
You lied.
Why?
Can you tell me why?
Maybe it was a game
I was blind.
I'm writing this.
Trying to unwind.
Drank to fast.
Trying to align
Myself with what you see as fine.
But it was a waste.
You water my time.
I gotta move on.
I gotta live my life.

Why Can't Nobody?

No, I really am tired of talking about it,
Even though I'm about to talk about it...
Why can't nobody love me?
Long paragraphs that start with
"I thought about you all night"
I can't say I know what that's like
I'd say I've had admirers, well not quite
I've had people chase me to get what's right
In between my thighs; get piped
No texts, no calls, no fight
I'm like alright; I'll just fly a kite
I really am tired of talking about it,
Even though I'm about to talk about it,
Why can't nobody love me?
I understand why they say
"I keep a ready clip"
Cause the torture is dangerous
Trying to trust, just makes me sick
Sometimes I just wanna finish it
Why can't nobody love me?
I look at it like a vacation home
Where people go but don't stay long
Because to them it's just a loan
They know they have a place to return
They can go home
No. I really am tired of talking about it
Even though I'm about to talk about it
Why can't nobody...see?

You know even when I compromise,
Give a little, ends in lies
Hold it in, no one tries
More cold nights
Lonely cries
I just wanna know if it's me?

Black Bird

I cried all the way to the cemetery, again
I couldn't find my worth in a plastic bag
I was so lost
No one loved me, he didn't want me
These two things I felt certain
They always say "You're never alone"
"Someone out there loves you".
&You think about it, and you know
It's probably true
But in the moment, these words do nothing
To fill the hole that's consuming you
& I was being consumed
I was tired of being abused
A penny with a hole in it
Sole-less shoes
So there I was, parked up at the cemetery
Crying like a new born child
I wept
Screaming and shouting
I wept
From all the secrets I kept
A black bird so damaged
She saw no hope that she could fly
So I cried for all those who are living and hurt me
& I cried for all of those who hurt me and died
Black bird, ugly black bird, how could I ever fly?

Psalms 56:8

A Black bird so damaged that
She could not see
That all her hopes and dreams
Could be fulfilled in thee
Black bird so damaged by
The dirt and the debris
Did not realize that whom the Son sets free
Is free indeed
No more captivity
Black bird spread your wings,
& walk in your liberty
It's true that you were wounded
But he was bruised for your iniquity
They hurt you,
That cannot be denied
But it's only dust, brush it off,
And fly
In him, you do NOT have to hide
Trade your sorrow for his pride
Take his hand; he will be your guide
Your wings were created for his glory
So black bird, mount up and take flight
You. Are. Not. Stained.
More like tie-dyed
Faith is taking the first step
When there is no clear vision in sight
All is not lost
Black bird, mount up and take flight

Psalms 56:8

Keep Yo I'm Sorry

Fuck you.
& you can keep your I'm sorry.
I already heard this story
& I'm over it.
The last chapter sucks ass.
So much for moving too fast
Maybe good things won't result from the past.
I stayed in class
Studied it all & still can't pass.
I already read this. & the last chapter is trash.
Heart break
an emotional crash.
Where I used to drown
I'll thrash.
I will not sink.

Let It Shine

2,4,6,8 plus one that's 9
You had 9 opportunities to rethink this crime
Young white male
Historic black church
Open fire
Ascended 9 lives
Media reads "It's not about race this time"
Then blame it on the light
It was too bright in evil's eye
They had to dim the light
Let it shine! Let it shine!
Let us breathe
We just need to breathe…
We can't wear hoodies
& we can't be young
Now there are new pretend rules
For little boys
With little pretend guns
They'll shoot!
Stop! Don't run!
They'll shoot!
Stand straight, Hands up
They'll shoot at you
They don't know if you're bending over to charge at them
Or if you bending over to tie your shoes
So they'll shoot…
Armed in red white and blue
They shoot…

Psalms 56:8

Yet race is not the issue
Blame it on the light
It was too bright in evil's eye
They have to dim the light
Let it shine! Let it shine!
Cause now we live in a time
Where you ain't even gotta rhyme
& you can run & have a stance in a political
Race
Where a toupee & a little cash is the new black face
Where selfies and "I wear my ego like my purse" is the new craze
Where we can watch children starve to death on day time television
& feel nothing cause we don't know how it taste....
We don't know the taste...
Cause if it ain't us about us?
Then it's a waste
How can we be free?
We desperately need to be free
If we begin to cleanse our hearts
Then maybe we'll see
The power to happiness is peace and unity
It lies within you & lies with in me
What you give is what you'll receive
I hope you hear me

2017

How Can I Tell You I love you?

How can I tell you I love you?
When I'm not sure if I can even correctly identify what that means.
I mean I miss you.
& I think of yu during the in between
At every beautiful scene
When the music's serene
I do. But how can I tell you I love you
When this world said that love is not a real thing.
That it's a choice, it's a fling.
That it takes a team.
Of side hoes and boyfriend #2 & no rings.
Worse than the super bowl you have to fight for this dream
The dream to love. But how can I tell you I love you if I heard from
grapevine that it would sting.
Then what do I do when you speak & the angels sing?
I didn't choose that, You know what I mean? It's just flows out of me when
I feel you, I flow upstream

Psalms 56:8

Between Me and You

I wish things could have gone more smoothly
Between me & you
Because no one else will share what we shared
Between me & you
I know I was over-protective at times
Between me & you
But that's only because I truly recognized the rareness
Between me & you
You spent so much time reminding me
& this is just between me & you
Of the importance of the friendship
Between me & you
When I came back around
Because of what you were going through
You said you'd never felt so connected to a person
I mean, is that true?
Or was that just between me & you too…
Cause for real I'm having a hard time understanding the sever
Between me & you
Can't really put a finger on it
What did we do?
What happened to the magic
Between me & you?
Cause at one point you were my star boy
I was the sun between the dark & you
What has pain done to me & you?
I wish things could have gone more slowly
Between me & you
Cause I wouldn't replace a millisecond of love
Between me & you

Psalms 56:8

Behind The Sunset With You

Behind the Sunset with you
Behind all of the colors
The orange & the blues
It is heaven...
I'm in heaven with you
There were so many times that I couldn't defend myself
But I always found the courage to stand up for you
Because when I was just scattered pieces
You were there & you were the glue
I know I can be loud & I know I haven't always been true
But I see infinity when I look at you
&, I just want to say thank you
Because it was behind the sunset
That I really felt you....
I've been so scared to lose you,
That's why I work as hard as I do
I'm scared that if I let up for a second
There'd be no more you
Because you are my sunset
You are my altitude
You are my warrior
You are my red & blue...It was after all the rain baby,
When all the material flew
It was there in the bareness
There was me & there was you
Because, you are my sunset
You're my honeydew
You are my evening star
You don't even have a clue

Psalms 56:8

I know I'm your lover
I just never thought I'd be who you'd choose
To be a part of such a beautiful portrait
The sunset that is you
& it is behind the sunset where you'll find me
I'll always be there for you
Because behind the sunset is the heaven
My home when I'm with you.

2.5

You couldn't even last 2.5 minutes
& you walking round here like we did it
Boy that ain't count
I spent more time with Niggas using their mouth
Talking to me like you gave a handout
Funny, Nigga you is funny
Chest puffed out, barking your demands like a child, nose running
Swearing there's no Cher to your Sonny
Baby, stop it, clean ya' sneakers, ya' looking a lil' bummy
I guess I could ask myself
Why I keep giving in to these dirty ass Niggas
If I'm so fly & work so hard
Why am I not entertaining Niggas with 6 figures
I guess cause we attract what we're used to
& who we attract is a reflection of who we think we deserve
I was headed down the highway of familiarity
& I finally hopped the curb.
Ya' heard?
Stepping my game up means you gotta step too
You ain't gonna be jumping on my emotions
This ain't Bounce U
Bounce...you...
You gotta bounce dude
Cause the minute I woke up
Is when I didn't hit snooze...
So take the remainder of those 5 minutes
& check out, you lose.

Psalms 56:8

Radiate

So that's what I'm going to do.
I'm going to radiate all my love around you…
& if you stay grandma,
I promise this too:
I promise to love myself better,
I shake the generational curses loose
I'll wear a jacket when it's chilly ….
I'll use a napkin when I eat my food…
& when I'm in the house I'll wear my house shoes…
That's exactly what I'm going to do
I'm going to radiate all my love around you
But if you go sweet lady
Softly bid your adieu
Your virtuous ascension into heaven
Oh god, what a miraculous debut.
If you leave you'll only lose pain
Everything you gain will be peaceful & new
So much love you've been giving me
I saved it & I'm sending it to you
Because Grandma I can't really explain it
You are the family glue
You are the pillar, the rock, the anchor
You are the chicken noodle soup!
No, I don't have any way to repay you
But here's what I know I can do
I'm going to sit with you each & every moment
& I'm going to radiate my love around you
I'm going to sit here right beside you…
& I'm going to radiate my love around you.

Psalms 56:8

Strange Fruit

Ohhh what you did to me
I was nothing short of unworthy
But I refuse to hang from the poplar tree
Because of your insecurities
NO.
You low down dirty nigga
With no job
You manipulating weak ass nigga
Can't afford it, so you rob
Thief
Taking from these women that you know you can't keep
Taking from their treasure like a sneaky monkey
NO.
Get your grubby hands off of her glory.
She is not yours and she will never be.
Good Bye to that victim mentality
Ohh what you did to me
Then pulled up a chair
To watch me bleed
Me, bleed, as you sowed the seed
Of destruction, shame, fear and controversy
Hoarder
Taking more than you eat
Piling everything up
For a never ending feast
I will not hang from the poplar tree
I will not die on your behalf
What about me?

Strange fruits that hang
& strange fruits that couldn't see
Died on the account of their abusers
You ain't killing me.
I'll cut you down strange fruits
& finally I'll be free
Ohhhh what you did to me
Made me who you could never be

White Elephant

There's a lot more going on than what we are willing to discuss…
The white elephant in the room…ready to spontaneously combust
We all need each other…yet we fight and we fuss
We say that we love God…but in whom do we trust?
We scream "Black Lives Matter!"
But pull back the white hoods…it's us killing us…
Tell me, where will we draw the line?
When they tear down our houses, to build more graves
Cause we're running out of time
How many murders will it take for y'all to realize?
It's not cool to die!
It's not cool to point guns at each other
And it's not cool to lie
It's not cool to pretend to be somebody you not
It's not cool making your family cry…
Cause then your only family tie
Will end with "Rest in Paradise"
With tearful eyes
Afraid to even question…did you sink or did you rise?
Crying "I believe in my heart they were saved"
Knowing your behaviors were on the dark side…
So there you'll lie…
6 feet under in the elephant cemetery
Buried with the same burden
The one's before you left to carry….
They don't want yall to go through this again
So promise me you'll hear me?
Dig up the bones in the elephant cemetery
Talk about how you feel with someone
If you love somebody get married
Bring back the love to the black community

Psalms 56:8

Dig up the bones in the elephant cemetery
Only we can save us
Dig up the bones in the elephant cemetery
Believe in the God you say you trust
& dig up the bones in the elephant cemetery.

Mighty Oak Tree

& she shall be like a tree…
Firmly planted by the streams of water
Which yields its fruits in it's season
& her leaf does not wither
& whatever she does
She prospers…

For she is a mighty oak tree
She's found her peace

Grandma mighty oak tree
That bows to the wind but does not cease
Swaying to the overcomers anthem
Dancing with the sea
Singing to the storm clouds
There is liberty
Some could say you're the tree of music
As each one of your branches move to a different beat
Some might call you Artist Arbol
From nothing, you created a masterpiece
Some might say a weeping willow…
For your children, you fell to your knees
A wisdom tree even
You knew who could supply your needs
& even when the wind was relentless
You never lost a leaf
& because of your strength
We can all see
That nothing can break a mighty oak tree
God protects the mighty oak tree

Psalms 56:8

Love Flows

You know how hard it was for me to write this?
You know they want poetry that's church appropriate!
Go ahead, laugh it up, I know you're getting a kick out of it
The cleanest thing I think you've ever said to me was
"Always keep a spare for the flat you're about to get"
& even that had a crazy meaning!
But I'll never forget,
Your quick wit & sarcastic responses
It was real work trying to keep up with all of you
If I'm being honest
& honestly, I want you to know
That even when you can't see it
Love flows….
Love flows & it has no end
& Love is forgiving and it doesn't pretend
Aunt Neissy, You are loved and you will be missed
& anyone who really got to see you. I mean
Really experience you was truly blessed.
Because, Love flows; Love flows and
Your love kept you going
& because of your love you took risk
To stay here….
To see your grandchildren grow
You fought to become closer to your children, so they'll always know
That love flows…
& that the vessel it uses is just that, a vessel
Love can flow through anything, in many ways, in any season
& That's the lesson.
They say we each love to the best of our own capabilities and even
when people push for us to have more to give, we're giving all we have
& I keep that close to me

Psalms 56:8

Because perfection was out of the question for you
& I admired that
You battled for your life
You battled to be who you were
But you never battled to get it right
Every single person is battling something we have
no idea about, let's keep that in plain sight.
Because the world is going to form an opinion
from what they think they know
& that's ok
As long as you know that love flows
& that God is love
& that we only get one life
So let the love flow.
For every person sitting here with me
It doesn't matter how broken you believe to be
YOU ARE A VESSEL
Set your love free
Know that the God who created you
Only operates in love, forgiveness, healing and peace
& if he didn't believe we deserved those things he wouldn't
Have created you or me
Give your pain to him
Cast upon him all your sorrow
Allow him the chance to show you
Just how much love flows...

Psalms 56:8

Give Up

I don't wanna do this…I don't wanna be depressed anymore, don't wanna feel worthless, don't wanna feel not good enough anymore…I don't wanna…give up

I don't wanna argue anymore. I don't wanna be rejected anymore, I don't wanna beg…I don't wanna give up.

I don't wanna be stressed anymore….I don't wanna be weighed down anymore…I don't wanna drown. I don't want to give up.

I don't wanna do this…I don't wanna be depressed anymore, don't wanna feel worthless, don't wanna feel not good enough anymore…I don't wanna…give up.

Remember when you said you supported me?

2018

Psalms 56:8

Born This Way

I do wish I was never born this way ...
In such a world of un-wanted-ness.
I was not wanted miss.
& I always knew that shit.
I always knew that shit.
They call you crazy
Convince you that your ideas are weak.
Your feelings are weak.
Blend in with the sheep.
But you always know.
Cause In the middle of the night
Here comes that hole...
& you dive in it.
& it consumes you.
Yet it soothes you.
Cause being alone is the only feeling not new to you.
Don't act like this is new to you.
You knew I wasn't supposed to be here.
Not like this, not this way
& you act like you have no clue why I act this way!!
But they didn't want me.
The cold world confronted me
Ma'am
Since birth, no safe place on this earth.
That hurts.
That shit hurts.

Psalms 56:8

Ma'ammm
I have no recollection of who I am
Only what I'm not
& that's not good enough.
Don't lie to me. I'm not good enough so let me do the shit I'm good enough
to do & that's nothing....
Don't you think, I wish I wasn't born this way?
I wish I wasn't born this way...

How Do You Want It?

You get tired of talking
Cause you know they're not listening
But they're always listening in on the things they hear about you.
You get tired of begging
Cause you know you don't really want free
But they still want you to be easy
Yet they want you to make them work for it.
Child I just don't get it. Do you want it easy or you want it hard?
Cause I done tried to play both parts.
& only ended up with a broken heart
Soooooooooooo
What's the secret?

I Don't Know What I'm doing For real

I don't know what I'm doing for real.
I just know somebody›s gotta protect me...
& I don't even do that great job at it.
Maybe I'm not ready to give myself away, to allow myself to be vulnerable with someone else. Especially if that person is not willing to be vulnerable with me. I don't know what I'm doing for real. I just know somebody's gotta protect me...somebody's gotta treat me right.
It seems like I love to easy, give a way to easy & get left or passed over easily too. It's like I rush to show my worth & I pray to put a spell on you.
Cause I don't want to lose
I'm scared that if you chose
Than you'll just cruise
Until you see
Whatever it is about me
That everyone else sees
& you Leave.
With out explaining
What it is about me that keeps them fleeing like I'm a disease.
I don't really know what I'm doing for real but somebody's gotta protect me. Somebody's gotta look out for me. In this world that's dog eat. & it's gotta be me. I look out for me.

Psalms 56:8

Shine in the Infinity

I'm NOT going to another funeral
I'm not fixing my lips to say Rest In Peace
Because, I know you're at peace
But I can't seem to find peace
It's like you're taking a piece of me…

I'm NOT going to another Funeral
So thank God this is a glamorous celebration
Because I received the revelation
That you are a rare constellation
& there's no replacing you…

I'm NOT going to your funeral Sheena,
But I'm right here at your Suarez
& we will sashay through the night in your memory
Because I remember what you said to me

"Bean, I refuse to let you fail. I've been there, felt that and I know you can
tell…I'm struggling right now, But there's a better place for me."
You said "I'm going to take the best in me & give it to you…& you take
it & pay it forward too…"
Sheena…there's no replacing you.

I'm not going to another funeral
So thank you for inviting me to this sensational event
I'm tired of saying "I would have never imagined"
But I just..would have never imagined this…
Like the story of the Capulets & the Montagues
How did Jay Z say it ? "Nobody wins when the family feuds"

Psalms 56:8

You were just so beautiful
Your heart entered the room before you
I know that God makes no mistakes
& there's a purpose to our fate
There is a purpose to our fate
I know God makes no mistakes

Such a beautiful tragedy
That tells a story of an alluring tapestry
Sometimes, the most broken hearts
Are hidden so craft fully
So candidly…
But we can miss the message
If we choose not to see
That we are so desperately
So overwhelmingly
In need of Gods healing touch
He knew us before we even existed
No sin is too much

So…since we are not at a funeral
Can God have this next dance?
Place your heart in his hands
& dance with your father again

He's not only calling for forgiveness
He's calling for release
Release your fractured heart
Release those negative thoughts

Psalms 56:8

Where the spirit of the Lord is
There is liberty
& like the Mighty Oak Tree
Love flows in an infinite stream
So, no...not,Rest In Peace
But, Shine in the infinity

Psalms 56:8

The One

Nothing seems real though,
Nobody feels real sometimes
It feels like I'm surrounded by people who just deal with me & pity my
brokenness,
They're not looking through the right lense
Like I'm always gonna be the poor one, the one who can't keep her mouth
shut, the one who doesn't fit in.
The one no one wants, the one who doesn't want herself…& I don't wanna
be her anyone more.
I don't wanna carry that sin.
The one who hides behind God, the one who feels like she's always in front
of an audience and her naked self isn't good enough to audition. Her truth
won't gain the acceptance.
The one who feels condemned
The one not comfortable in her own skin
The victim
The one always waiting for her unexpected, yet expected end.
So consumed with waiting to die, blind to that fact that she's not even
living.
I don't want to be her.
I don't want to be her again.
This time I want to win
I want to let the thoughts come freely
Maybe they'll slow down then
I wanna let people say & think what they wanna think
& trust that they have no hell to put me in
I wanna sing to the music inside me
No longer will I be in contempt
Of the rigid, toxic, judicial system
Of my mind that I took residence in

I wanna be free like the butterfly
I wanna be like the pollen caught up in the wind
I want I stretch towards the sky like the sunflower
Most importantly, I don't wanna give in
I wanna live
I wanna live
I wanna live